Creative Techniques

for Stained Glass

CLIFF KENNEDY AND JANE WENDLING POMPILIO

NORTH LIGHT BOOKS
CINCINNATI, OHIO
www.artistsnetwork.com

Dedication

*To our families and friends
who have supported and encouraged us
throughout our lives
and have made life worth living.*

Other fine North Light Books are available from your local bookstore, art supply store or direct from the publisher.

08 07 06 05 04   5 4 3 2 1

Library of Congress Cataloging-in-Publication Data
Kennedy, Cliff
Creative techniques for stained glass / Cliff Kennedy and Jane Wendling Pompilio.
    p. cm.
Includes index.
ISBN 1-58180-604-3 (pbk. : alk. paper)
    1. Glass craft. 2. Glass painting and staining. I. Pompilio, Jane Wendling, 1952-
    II. Title.
TT298.K465 2004
748.5'028--dc22
                                                    2004052085

Editor: Jennifer Fellinger
Cover Designer: Marissa Bowers
Interior Designer and Layout Artist: Cynthia Patten Stanard
Production Coordinator: Sara Dumford
Photographers: Christine Polomsky, Al Parrish and Tim Grondin
Photo Stylist: Jan Nickum

Metric Conversion Chart		
To convert	to	multiply by
Inches	Centimeters	2.54
Centimeters	Inches	0.4
Feet	Centimeters	30.5
Centimeters	Feet	0.03
Yards	Meters	0.9
Meters	Yards	1.1
Sq. Inches	Sq. Centimeters	6.45
Sq. Centimeters	Sq. Inches	0.16
Sq. Feet	Sq. Meters	0.09
Sq. Meters	Sq. Feet	10.8
Sq. Yards	Sq. Meters	0.8
Sq. Meters	Sq. Yards	1.2
Pounds	Kilograms	0.45
Kilograms	Pounds	2.2
Ounces	Grams	28.3
Grams	Ounces	0.035

About the Authors

Cliff Kennedy owns and operates Kaleidoscope Stained Glass in the MainStrasse Village of Covington, Kentucky. After perfecting his art glass hobby, Cliff opened his studio doors for retail sales, commissioned work, restoration of stained and beveled glass, and hands-on instructional classes. He also has taught classes at Northern Kentucky University. Proud to be a Marine and the father of three sons, Cliff enjoys his creative profession during the week and drag racing on the weekends.

Cliff's latest style, called "Funky Art Glass," can be viewed on his web site, www.stainedglass4you.com, where he accepts commissions from around the world. Also featured on this web site are seven stained glass pattern books published by Kaleidoscope for the stained glass industry.

Jane Wendling Pompilio, a former elementary school teacher, is a mom to Lauren and two Jasons (one a son-in-law). Always with pencil in hand and eager to create, Jane has found Kaleidoscope to be a haven for developing and creating new stained glass designs. Teaching art glass classes and spending time with new friends from all walks of life and from all over the world have made her experience at Kaleidoscope a special treasure.

Acknowledgments

A special thank you to **Debra Neace** whose creativity, hard work and artistic talent help make Kaleidoscope Stained Glass a highly respected studio for beveled and art glass restoration and commissioned windows.

And to Vinson Neace, who has worked diligently to create thousands of iron products for Kennedy/Kaleidoscope.

Thank you to Mark and Angie Hubbard, whose knowledge and talent motivate them to work tirelessly to make business grow in new directions.

And thanks to our new friends, Tricia Waddell, our great Editorial Director; Christine Doyle and Jenny Fellinger, our awesome editors; and Christine Polomsky for her extraordinary photography andendless encouragement.

We thank all of you for giving us another wonderful experience that we will never forget!

Table
of Contents

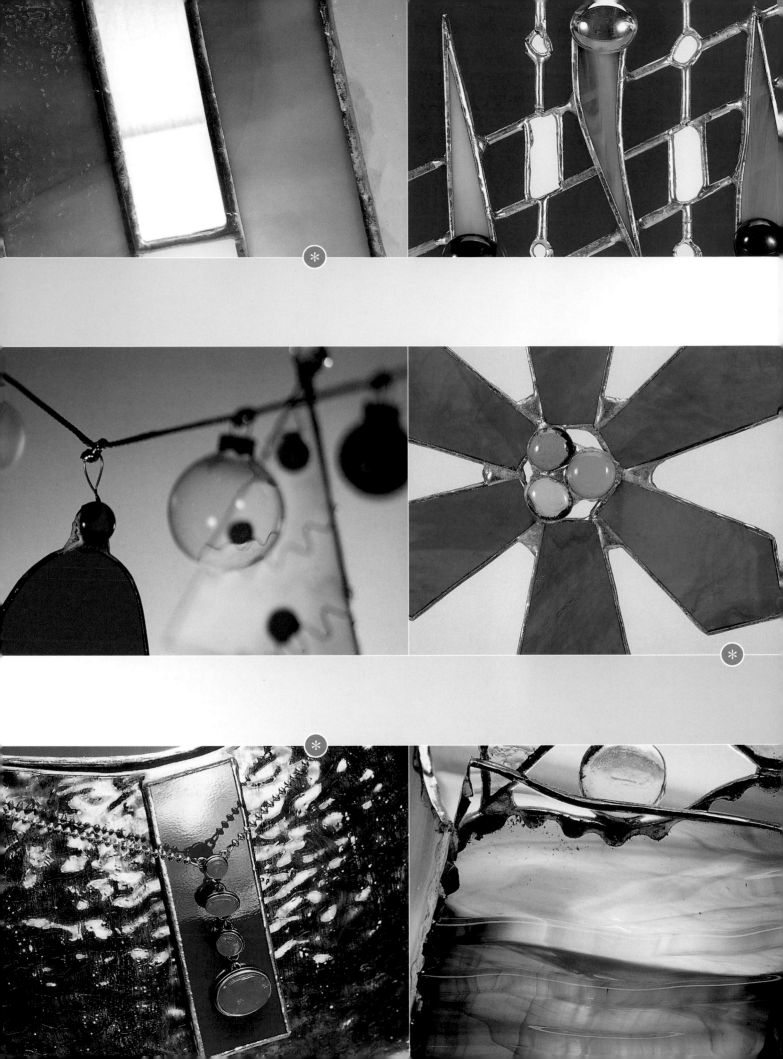

Introduction

The power of color is undeniable. As human beings, we naturally respond to specific colors with a wide range of emotions, whether we are conscious of it or not. It is no surprise, then, that most people are moved by the wonderfully luminous, colorful art of stained glass.

Throughout history, stained glass has been celebrated as a unique instrument of color. Though a stained glass object may last for hundreds of years, its appearance is ever-changing in relation to the light that filters through it. As you gaze at a stained glass window, its colors may inspire warmth and comfort, excitement and exhilaration, calm and peacefulness, or wonder and amazement. If you view the very same window at another time of day or season, its colors may evoke a completely different feeling. Part of the allure of stained glass is this dynamic power, this ability to renew itself generation after generation as a beautiful and powerful art form. Perfected through the ages, stained glass holds as much appeal today as it did centuries ago.

In our stained glass studio, we have forty-five years of combined experience in the restoration of old stained glass windows and the construction of new ones. So, the techniques that we have presented in this book combine the old with the new. Some designs follow traditional construction methods, particularly the copper foil technique established a century ago by the famed stained glass artist Louis Comfort Tiffany. Others incorporate beads and wire to create a modern, updated look. No matter what the style, it is the radiant colored glass that makes every project sing! Whether you prefer traditional or contemporary style, you are sure to find many colorful projects that suit your taste.

As instructors, it is our goal to spread the joy of stained glass by fostering an appreciation for the art form in our students. To inspire you, we used our imagination to create small-scale, dimensional designs that are both functional and gorgeous. Tested in our classroom, most projects are beginner friendly. Some require only a few hours to complete, and most can be created in a weekend. Make one for yourself and one as a gift that is sure to please any friend!

Materials and Tools

The art of stained glass requires certain materials and tools, some of which may be familiar to you and others which may not. Most of these supplies can be purchased at stained glass shops, hobby stores, hardware stores and related web sites. Check your local phone book for stained glass sources in your area.

Every project in this book begins with a list of required tools and materials. Be sure to check that you have everything on the list before you begin. The first step to creating beautiful stained glass is knowing how to use the supplies, so take the time to familiarize yourself with all your materials.

Glass

Glass is the most basic—and no doubt the most beautiful—material you'll be using. With variations in glass color, texture and density, your options seem almost endless!

Stained glass is often defined by its opacity, or the degree to which it allows the passage of light. There are three primary degrees of opacity: transparent, opaque and translucent (also called semiopaque and semitransparent). Transparent glass allows light to pass through it completely, opaque glass allows very little or no light through it, and translucent glass admits some light through it.

Baroque glass combines clear glass with one or two colors in a swirling pattern.

Cathedral glass is a colored transparent glass, often consisting of a single color.

Cat's paw glass is an opalescent glass (see next column), characterized by a mottled pattern resembling the paw prints of a cat.

Granite glass has rough, pebbly ridges on one side of the glass.

Hammered glass features a repetitive, uniform pattern of small, circular knobs, resembling strokes from a hammer.

Iridized glass has a shiny surface that, when struck by light, resembles oil on water. The iridescent surface creates a rainbowlike effect, changing colors with the angle at which light hits it.

Mottled glass has irregular spots of translucent color in circular patterns. Mottled glass is typically varied in color, density and texture.

Muffle glass has a bumpy texture, with a highly refractive and crystalline surface.

Opalescent glass is semi-opaque, characterized by a milky appearance. The glass can be composed of one color or many colors, but the color is usually dense, sometimes including transparent areas.

Ripple glass features a regular rippled texture.

Streaky glass features two or more colors, unevenly distributed in streaks or swirls.

Water glass has a texture which, when struck by light, looks like ripples on water.

Beveled glass has a surface with interior corners cut at an angle and finished.

Glass nuggets are small, rounded pieces of stained glass that vary in size.

Basic Materials

In addition to glass, you will need the following basic materials for most projects. Some projects require additional materials that are not included below; be sure to check the specific project list before beginning.

A **wooden work surface** with a minimum 1/2" (13mm) thickness is best for assembling and soldering stained glass objects. The surface should be large enough to support the overall size of the finished product, and it should be located near electrical outlets and a faucet.

Paper patterns, provided in the introduction of each project, will make cutting and assembling glass easy.

Household scissors are used to cut the outside perimeter of paper patterns.

Pattern shears are special three-bladed scissors designed specifically for cutting apart stained glass patterns. We recommend copper foil shears, which remove a strip of paper between the pattern pieces to allow for the width of copper foil seams.

Spray adhesive keeps pattern pieces in place while the glass is being cut.

Low-tack tape or masking tape and a marker are used to label glass pieces.

Copper foil tape is an adhesive-backed foil that is wrapped around the edges of glass pieces before soldering. Copper foil tape is available in a range of widths; 7/32" (5mm) is preferable but 1/4" (6mm) is also acceptable. It is also available with a wavy decorative edge and with a black or silver backing.

Liquid flux is a chemical substance that is applied to copper foil before soldering. Flux allows the hot solder to fuse to the copper foil surface.

A **flux brush** is used to apply flux to copper foil surfaces.

Solder is a mixture of metals, most often tin and lead, used to join stained glass pieces. When applied to copper foil, hot solder melts and creates a sturdy seam that holds the glass pieces together. We recommend using mixtures of either 63% tin and 37% lead or 60% tin and 40% lead.

Brass hangers are hanging devices with hooks that can easily be soldered to the back of stained glass pieces.

continued next page

Patina is a chemical that, when applied to a finished piece, changes the natural color of the soldered surface to a copper, brass or black color. Always wear gloves when using patina, and always follow the instructions provided on the bottle.

Tinned wire, available in different gauge strengths, is used as a decorative element in many of the projects. The wire must be tinned for solder to adhere to it.

Zinc channel is a metal strip that is used to frame stained glass pieces. The strip features either a U-shaped or an H-shaped groove into which the glass is inserted. The width of the frame, which covers the perimeter edge of the stained glass piece, varies; 1/8" (3mm) and 3/8" (10mm) widths are used in several projects.

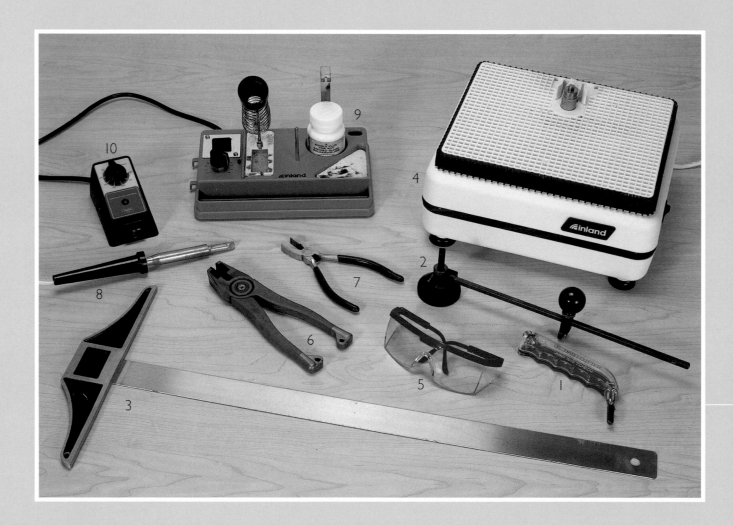

BASIC TOOLS
(1) pistol-grip glass cutter; (2) circle cutter; (3) straightedge; (4) electric glass grinder; (5) protective eyewear; (6) running pliers; (7) grozing pliers; (8) soldering iron; (9) iron station; (10) temperature control

Basic Tools

Listed below are the basic tools needed for most projects. Some projects call for additional tools that are not described below; be sure to check the specific project list before beginning.

A **pistol-grip glass cutter** is our choice tool for cutting glass. With a built-in oil reservoir, it features a self-oiling cutting wheel and an easy-to-hold acrylic pistol-grip handle. The cutter scores the glass with a "zipping" sound, weakening the glass for easy, controlled breakage.

A **circle cutter** is a glass cutter designed specifically for cutting circles.

A **straightedge** can be used as a guide when cutting glass. Some straightedges, such as rulers and T-squares, have a lip that aids in steady positioning.

An **electric glass grinder** features a diamond-coated grinding head that rotates against the edge of the glass to smooth out sharp, jagged edges. The glass grinder creates clean, even edges, which allows the glass pieces in a pattern to fit together more precisely. As the glass runs against the grinding head, a sponge, kept wet by a reservoir of water inside the machine, prevents glass particles from being released. Always wear protective eyewear and remove any jewelry when using the grinder. Follow the manufacturer's directions to service the machine.

Protective eyewear, such as safety glasses or goggles, should be worn at all times to prevent eye injuries.

Running pliers assist in the controlled breakage of glass along score lines. These pliers have a set of curved, padded jaws, which feature a central guide mark on the top jaw.

Grozing pliers assist in the controlled breakage of glass that is more difficult to cut, such as small or severely curved pieces. Made specifically for working with glass, these pliers have spring tension handles and curved, serrated jaws for gripping glass.

A **soldering iron** is the instrument used to melt and apply solder. A 100-watt iron with a chisel tip provides consistent heat for smooth, easy soldering.

An **iron station** keeps all the basic soldering tools accessible. It includes a coiled wire iron holder, a no-spill flux bottle holder and a flux brush holder.

A **temperature control** is a phaser that maintains a selected temperature by regulating the flow of current to the soldering iron.

SAFETY TIP

Electrical equipment and chemical products require special care when using them. When working with glass grinders and soldering irons and when handling flux and patina, be sure to follow the instructions provided by the manufacturer. This will keep your supplies in good working condition and will ensure your own safety.

Basic Techniques

The intricate appearance of stained glass design often fools people into thinking it is a complicated art form only to be undertaken by true masters. In fact, stained glass techniques are easy to learn, and you don't need years of experience or a sophisticated workshop to create impressive objects. You just need a work surface, a few tools and a little practice—and you'll be on your way to becoming a skilled stained glass artist yourself!

There are four basic steps to completing a stained glass piece: choosing and preparing the glass; scoring and cutting the glass into individual pieces; readying the glass pieces for soldering; and soldering, or physically joining, the pieces into a single unit. Don't be intimidated by the prospect of learning new techniques, such as cutting glass and soldering. Easily mastered, these techniques are essential to the stained glass process.

SAFETY TIP

For your own safety, follow these guidelines:

- When working with solder, flux and adhesives, always work in a well-ventilated area.

- Always wear safety goggles when you are cutting glass, using a glass grinder or soldering.

STEP ONE: Selecting and Preparing the Glass

In this book, we recommend specific colors and kinds of glass for each project. (To familiarize yourself with the different kinds of glass, refer to *Materials and Tools*, page 8.) Keep in mind, however, that there is no right or wrong combination of glass. Glass can be mixed and matched, and there are no rules dictating how this should be done. Perhaps you feel inspired to choose different glass, or perhaps your choices are determined by a limited availability of glass. In either case, feel free to substitute your choice of glass for our recommendations.

TIP

Although the colors you choose needn't match their environment, consider the surroundings in which the object will be placed as you select your colors. If you are seeking inspiration elsewhere, look no further than your backyard. Observe how colors mix in nature, then create a similarly harmonious palette. It's sure to be magnificent!

Consider how the glass functions in your design. If, for example, the glass represents water, use swirled glass that gives the look of waves. If the composition includes the sky, select glass that has the appearance of clouds. You can also incorporate nuggets and bevels for dimensional and prismatic effects.

Choose glass
When selecting your glass, view it in natural light to get a true sense of the color, the density and the texture.

Preparing Glass for Cutting

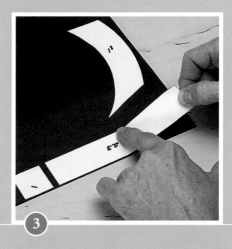

| ① | ② | ③ |

Cut pattern apart

Make two photocopies of the pattern (unless otherwise instructed), enlarging as directed in the pattern caption. Use household scissors to cut along the outside perimeter of one copy of the pattern, then use copper foil shears to cut the pattern apart into individual pieces. When you are finished, you should have several pieces, each labeled with a number. Use the color key accompanying the pattern to determine the color of glass needed for each numbered piece, then organize the pieces into groups according to color.

Spray adhesive on glass

Spray a thin, even coat of adhesive on the smoother side of the glass. Do not overspray, as you will not be able to peel the pattern pieces from the glass if the coat of adhesive is too heavy.

Affix pattern pieces to glass

Affix the cut pattern pieces to the glass. For pieces with straight edges or right angles, position the straight edges right along the edge of the glass. For curved or irregularly shaped pieces, position the piece at least ¼" (6mm) from the edge of the glass.

TIP

Copper foil pattern shears maintain proper size and proportion in the pattern by accounting for the copper foil channel between each piece of glass. This channel will later become a seam when it is soldered. Copper foil shears allow for a tight channel between glass pieces, which will result in a thin solder line. If you prefer a wider solder line, lead pattern shears allow for a wider channel between glass pieces.

STEP TWO: Cutting the Glass

When you use a glass cutter to "cut" glass, the cutting wheel does not actually penetrate the surface of the glass. Rather, it creates a score line, causing a weakness in the glass that allows for a clean, controlled break. You may want to practice making score lines on scrap glass until you feel comfortable holding the cutter and making the break.

Cutting Pieces with Straight Edges and Right Angles

Score glass

Hold the glass cutter at a 90° angle to the glass. With your free hand, hold a ruler or T-square along a perimeter edge of the pattern piece. Start at the bottom edge of the glass and slide the glass cutter forward, using the ruler as your guide to follow the cut as closely to the pattern edge as possible. Listen for a scratching or "zipping" sound that indicates a good score line. Follow the cut all the way through to the top edge.

Position running pliers

Grip the edge of the glass lightly with running pliers, aligning the central guideline on the top jaw of the pliers with the score line.

TIP

Make the score in one steady movement, and stop scoring only when you reach the opposite edge of the glass. Never stop cutting in the middle of a score. Also, do not try to rescore by going over the score line twice. This will damage the glass cutter, and it will not improve your score line.

Break glass

Apply light pressure to the handle of the pliers. The glass should break in a clean, straight cut along the score line.

Cutting Pieces with Curves

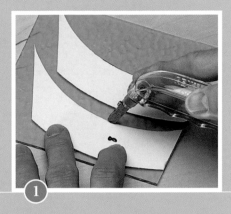
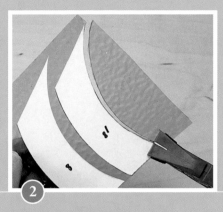
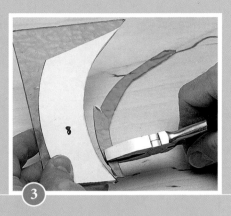

① **②** **③**

Score glass

Hold the glass cutter at a 90° angle to the glass, and position the cutting wheel right along the perimeter of the pattern piece. Start at the bottom edge or corner and slide the glass cutter forward, following along the perimeter edge as closely as possible. Listen for a scratching or "zipping" sound that indicates a good score line. Follow the cut all the way through to the opposite edge or to the next score line.

Position pliers and break glass

Lightly grip the edge of the glass with running pliers, aligning the central guideline on the top jaw of the pliers with the score line. Apply light pressure to the handle of the pliers. The glass should break in a clean cut along the score line.

Use grozing pliers for smaller pieces

To remove smaller pieces of glass from the edges, score as usual but use grozing pliers instead of running pliers to break the glass at the score line. With grozing pliers, grip the glass at a corner, apply gentle pressure and bend down at a slight angle until the piece breaks at the score line. Run the head of the grozing pliers along the cut edge of the glass to smooth out any rough or jagged edges.

TIP

You will find it much easier to cut curves if, when affixing a curved pattern piece on the glass prior to cutting, you do not position it too close to the edge of the glass.

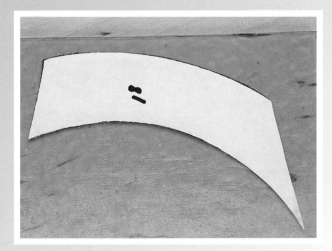
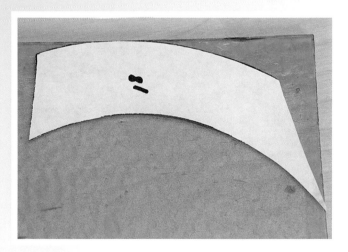

A curved pattern piece affixed at least ¼" (6mm) from the edge of the glass will cut and break easier... than a piece affixed right on the edge of the glass.

SAFETY TIP

To avoid injury and to avoid scratching good glass, clean your work surface with a bench brush after cutting each piece of glass.

Cutting Difficult Pieces

1

2

Score glass and tap to break

When cutting severe curves, you can tap the glass to break it rather than using pliers. First, score the glass with a glass cutter, then hold the glass in one hand and, with the other hand, use the ball of the glass cutter to tap on the underside of the glass, directly under the scored line. Continue tapping until a fracture occurs, then break the glass. This technique can also be used on thicker glass that is more difficult to break.

Or score and remove segments

For an especially deep curve, score and break away the glass in small, curved segments. After scoring the first curve, use the grozing pliers to grip one side of the curve. Apply gentle pressure until the glass begins to fracture, then grip the other side of the curve to complete the break. Continue to remove the scored glass piece by piece until you achieve the desired cut.

TIP

While circles can be cut using a regular glass cutter, a circle cutter makes the job much easier. The circle cutter has a suction cup that adheres to the glass as the radial arm pivots to score a circle.

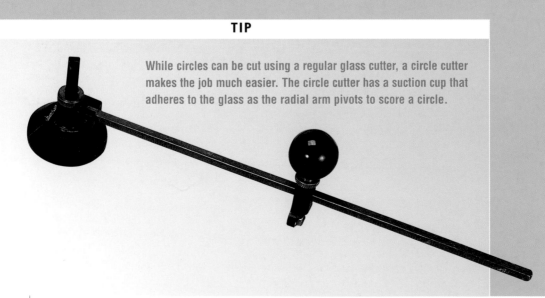

STEP THREE: Priming the Glass Pieces

After cutting all the glass, the next step is to prepare the glass pieces for the soldering process. For the best results, the pieces should fit together as tightly and as precisely as possible before they are joined with soldering. Grinding the glass ensures such precision, while labeling the glass provides mistake-free assembly. Once the glass is ground and labeled, it is primed for soldering with copper foil adhesive and liquid flux.

Grinding and Labeling Glass

Grind glass

Lay the piece of glass on the grid surface of the grinding machine. Turn the machine on; then, slowly and with a single motion, run each edge of the glass along the grinding wheel. Grind the glass until the edges are smooth and match the edges of the affixed pattern. Even if you achieve a precise cut with the glass cutter, you should still pass the piece through the grinder to smooth out the edges.

Remove adhesive residue

Soak the glass pieces in warm water for 10–15 minutes. Peel the adhered pattern paper from only one piece, removing all adhesive residue. Dry the piece of glass with a towel.

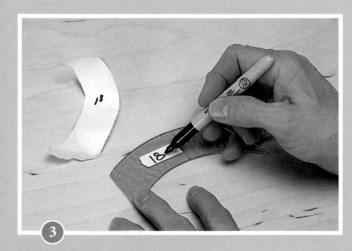

Label each piece of glass

Label the piece of glass with its corresponding number, using a marker and low-tack or masking tape. Repeat steps 2 and 3 for the remaining pieces until all the glass has been labeled.

Wrapping Copper Foil

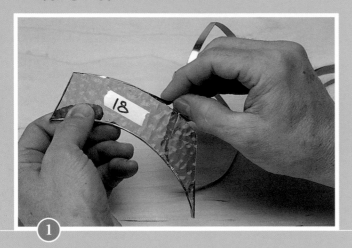

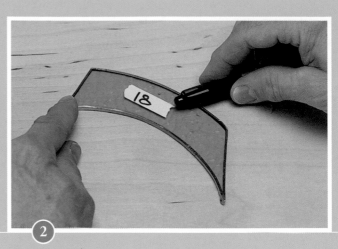

Wrap copper foil around glass

Wipe the edges of the glass with a cloth to remove any residue. Center the edge of the glass piece on the copper foil strip, then run the foil along the edge of the glass all the way around the piece. Overlap the foil slightly at the ends. Fold the foil down neatly and evenly onto both sides of the glass.

Burnish copper foil

Use the side of a pen, pencil or marker to smooth and burnish the foil, mitering the corners.

Applying Flux

Position pieces on top of pattern

Lay the numbered pieces of glass over the duplicate copy of the pattern, making sure that the number on the glass piece matches the number on the pattern piece. If the design has 90° corners, use a T-square to line up the perimeter corners at right angles. After aligning the perimeter, arrange the inside pieces with the pattern, fitting them together as tightly as possible. Regardless of how the inside pieces fit together, the outside pieces should always line up with the pattern perimeter.

Apply flux

Using a flux brush, apply flux liberally over all copper foiled areas. (Flux will not damage the glass.) Solder will adhere to the foil only if flux has been applied, so be sure to cover all copper foil surfaces. If you inadvertently knock any of the glass pieces out of place while applying flux, reposition them before moving on to the next step. Because flux is mildly corrosive, use caution when using it; keep your hands away from your eyes and mouth after using flux until you have washed your hands.

STEP FOUR: Soldering

Soldering is the means by which all the glass pieces are united to form a beautiful finished product. There are three main soldering techniques: *tack soldering, flat soldering* and *bead soldering*. All pieces must first be joined by tack soldering before they are secured and finished with flat soldering or bead soldering. When soldering, always start at the upper-left corner of the object and work down.

Tack solder

Holding the length of solder to the tip of the soldering iron, bring both the solder and the tip down to the copper foil. Allow a drop of solder to fall on top of the foil seam. Continue applying single drops of solder at random points along the seams, particularly on joints where several pieces meet, until all the pieces are secured to one another.

Flat solder or bead solder

To flat solder, pull the soldering iron along the copper foil seam, keeping the iron in contact with the foil to heat it as you apply the solder in a steady flow. Pull the solder continuously from one joint to the next, applying just enough solder to result in a thin layer on the copper foil. After the initial application, go over the seams to touch them up, flattening the solder, filling in any gaps and covering any exposed copper. To bead solder, pull the soldering iron along the copper foil as you would when flat soldering, only more slowly, allowing solder to build up, or bead, on the seam.

Wash piece and add patina

When the soldering job is complete, wash the finished piece in warm, soapy water to remove flux and labels, then dry with a soft cloth. The application of patina, shown above, is always optional. Patina gives the soldered surfaces an aged appearance with a black, copper or brass finish. (See *Tip* on page 95 for more about patina.) If you desire this look, apply patina with a brush, carefully following the instructions provided on the bottle. Wash the piece again in warm, soapy water and dry.

TIP

Tack soldering (1) holds glass pieces in place before you proceed with further soldering. Flat soldering (2) sometimes called *tinning*, fills the copper foil channel with melted solder and creates a flat seam. Bead soldering (3) builds up additional solder along a seam to create a rounded, dimensional effect.

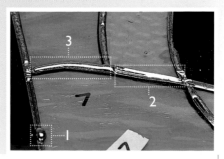

Antique Flower Window

In medieval times, when magnificent gothic churches were being built across Europe, stained glass became an important element of church décor. The glass served as a connection between earth, upon which the building stood, and heaven, from which the light came to illuminate the interior. Today, stained glass is everywhere, used to decorate far more environments than just churches—and its beauty is as breathtaking now as it was hundreds of years ago.

This design represents a small segment of a larger stained glass church window. Recently uncovered after ten years in storage, the newly restored window will soon be unveiled to church parishioners as part of a huge restoration project.

TOOLS AND MATERIALS

- pattern (2 copies)
- wooden work surface
- household scissors
- copper foil shears
- glass: red muffle, gold muffle, green muffle, turquoise muffle, dark blue muffle, violet muffle (refer to pattern for sizes)
- spray adhesive
- low-tack or masking tape
- marker

- pistol-grip glass cutter
- circle cutter (optional)
- grozing pliers
- running pliers
- electric glass grinder
- copper foil
- pen, pencil or marker
- T-square
- flux brush
- liquid flux

- solder
- soldering iron, with iron station and temperature control
- 5' (1.5m) zinc U-channel, ⅛" (3mm) width
- V-notcher (available at stained glass shops)
- horseshoe nails
- hammer
- 2 brass hangers
- soapy water and soft cloth
- patina

Preparation

Cut a copy of the pattern apart with household scissors and copper foil shears, spray the glass with adhesive, then affix the individual pattern pieces to the appropriate glass. Score the glass along the edges of the adhered paper and break the glass at the score line. Use a glass grinder to smooth out the edges of the glass pieces. Soak the pieces in warm water and remove the paper, then label each piece with its corresponding number, using low-tack tape and a marker. For a more detailed explanation, see *Basic Techniques*, pages 12–17.

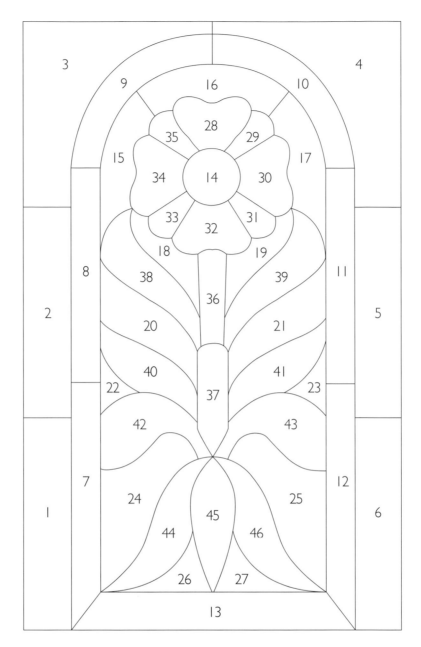

ANTIQUE FLOWER WINDOW PATTERN

Enlarge this pattern by 250% using a photocopier. Make two copies. (Some photocopiers only enlarge up to 200%. If this is the case, make a copy of the pattern at 200%, then photocopy that copy at 125%.)

Color Key

Use this key to select your glass, or choose your own palette instead. Listed below are the glass colors used in the project, followed by the corresponding pattern piece numbers.

- *red muffle: 7, 8, 9, 10, 11, 12, 13, 14*
- *gold muffle: 1, 2, 3, 4, 5, 6*

- *green muffle: 38, 39, 40, 41, 42, 43, 44, 45, 46*
- *turquoise muffle: 15, 16, 17, 18, 19, 20, 21, 22, 23, 24, 25, 26, 27*
- *dark blue muffle: 36, 37*
- *violet muffle: 28, 29, 30, 31, 32, 33, 34, 35*

1 Prepare glass

Cut, grind and label the glass. Wrap each piece of glass with copper foil.

2 Burnish copper foil

Burnish the copper foil using the side of a pen, pencil or marker.

3 Position glass and apply flux

Position the glass pieces on top of the pattern, using a T-square to line up the outside edges at right angles. Brush flux onto all copper foil areas.

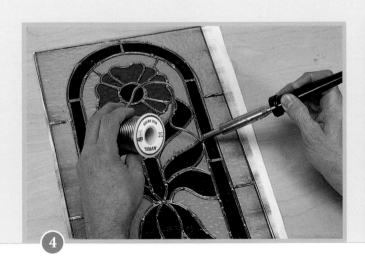

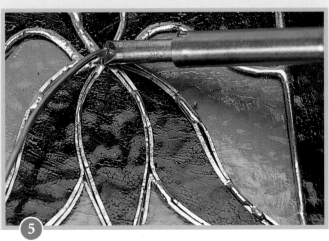

4 Tack solder

Tack solder the foiled pieces of glass together at random points along the copper foil seams until all pieces are joined.

5 Bead solder

Starting at the top left, bead solder the pieces of glass together along the copper foil seams. To allow room for the frame, stop soldering 1/8"–1/4" (3mm–6mm) from the outside edge. Turn the piece over, apply flux and solder the seams on the back side. Smooth out any imperfections using the solder and soldering iron.

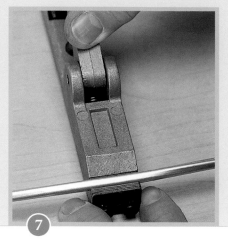

6

Begin wrapping channel around glass

Starting at one corner, wrap the zinc U-channel around the outside perimeter of the piece. When you get to the first corner, mark the channel with a marker.

7

Finish wrapping channel around glass

Use the V-notcher to cut a notch where you marked the corner, then bend the zinc channel to fit around the corner. Repeat for the remaining corners. When you have wrapped the channel all the way around the perimeter, use a permanent marker to mark the end. Use the notcher to make the final notch at this point. (See *Tip* below for more information about V-notchers.)

8

Break off remaining channel

Bend the zinc channel at the final notch and break off to remove the excess channel.

TIP

The V-notcher is a tool that facilitates the bending of zinc channel when you are making a frame for a stained glass window. To use the notcher, place the zinc in the slot, align the tool's groove to the mark you have made on the channel, then press the top handle down to create a sharp V-notch. The zinc should bend with ease at the notch.

Horseshoe nails are flat-sided nails that, when hammered gently into a wooden work surface, hold the glass flush against the metal channel or frame until soldering is complete.

Both V-notchers and horseshoe nails are available at stained glass shops.

9

Brace channel against glass

Lay the piece down on the wooden work surface. Around the outside perimeter of the zinc channel, gently hammer horseshoe nails into the wooden surface. The nails should butt against the zinc channel, holding it flush against the glass until the piece is completely soldered. Avoid placing nails at any joints where the soldered seams meet the channel.

Apply flux to channel

Brush flux onto all the joints where the soldered seams meet the zinc channel.

Solder joints along channel

Solder all the soldered seams to the zinc channel, securing the glass in the frame.

Solder joints along channel on reverse side

Turn the piece over, apply flux and solder all the soldered seams to the zinc channel on the back side.

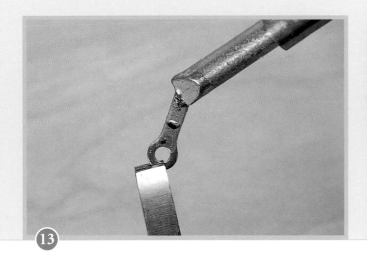

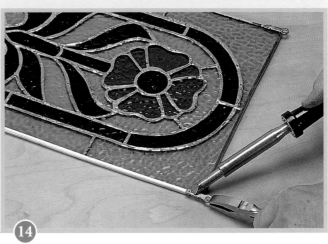

Tin hangers

Brush the brass hangers with flux, then tin the hangers, covering them with a thin layer of solder to make them the same color as the soldered areas. (See *Tip* on page 29 for more information about tinning surfaces.)

Attach hangers

Lay the hangers along the zinc channel at the top back corners so that only the hook extends beyond the top edge. Holding the hook in place with grozing pliers, brush flux onto the hangers and the corners, then solder a hanger to each corner. Clean the window with soapy water to remove flux, then dry with a soft cloth. Following the package instructions, apply patina to the frame and all soldered areas. Clean again with warm, soapy water, then dry.

Decorative Squares
Mirror

Stained glass objects do not have to be complicated to be beautiful; sometimes an ordinary shape is all the inspiration you need. The decorative motif in this charming mirror is a simple square, repeated around the perimeter to frame your reflection. Because every square is the same size, no complex glass cutting is required.

Choose glass with different textures in varying shades of red, gold, orange and purple. Or, go with cooler colors instead, using green, blue and aqua squares. No matter what palette you select, you're sure to smile when you look in this mirror and see the face of a promising stained glass artist!

TOOLS AND MATERIALS

* pattern (multiple copies, as directed)
* wooden work surface
* household scissors
* 6" x 11" (15cm x 28cm) mirror
* glass: red, orange, gold and purple in varied textures; cut into eighteen 1¾" (5cm) squares
* spray adhesive
* pistol-grip glass cutter

* grozing pliers
* running pliers
* electric glass grinder
* copper foil
* pen, pencil or marker
* flux brush
* liquid flux
* solder

* soldering iron, with iron station and temperature control
* 4' (1.3m) zinc U-channel, ⅛" (3mm) width
* V-notcher (available at stained glass shops)
* horseshoe nails
* hammer
* soapy water and soft cloth
* patina (optional)

Preparation

Cut out eighteen copies of the 1¾" (5cm) square pattern with household scissors, spray the glass with adhesive, then affix the individual pattern pieces to the appropriate colored glass. Score the glass along the edges of the adhered paper and break the glass at the score line. Use a glass grinder to smooth out the edges of the glass pieces. Soak the pieces in warm water and remove the paper. For a more detailed explanation, see *Basic Techniques*, pages 12–17.

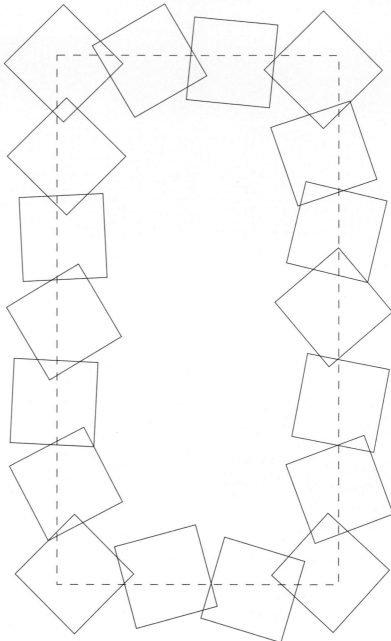

SQUARE TEMPLATE
Make eighteen copies.

DECORATIVE SQUARE MIRROR PATTERN
Enlarge this pattern by 200% using a photocopier. Make one copy.

Color Key

There is no set order for how the colors appear on the border of this mirror. If you have enough variations in color and texture, alternate the squares so there are no identical pieces next to each other.

Prepare glass

Cut and grind eighteen 1¾" (5cm) squares of glass. Wrap each piece of glass with copper foil, then burnish the foil.

Apply flux and tin edges

With a flux brush, apply flux to all copper foil areas. Tin the copper foil edges on all glass pieces.

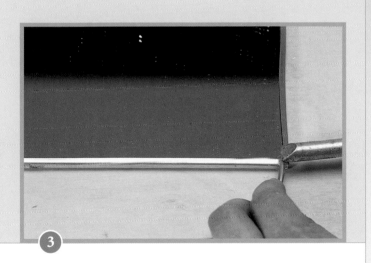

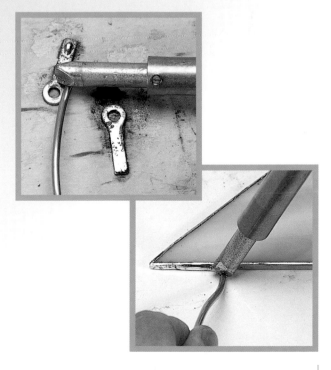

Wrap channel around mirror

Starting at one corner, wrap the zinc U-channel around the outside perimeter of the mirror. When you get to the first corner, mark the channel with a marker. Use the V-notcher to notch the channel at the mark, then bend the notched channel to fit around the corner. Repeat for the remaining corners. Wrap the channel all the way around the perimeter, then mark the point at which the channel should end. Make the finishing notch at this point. Bend the channel at the final notch and break off the excess. Gently hammer horse-shoe nails into the wooden work surface along the perimeter of the mirror to hold the channel flush against the mirror until the piece is secure. Solder each corner to seal and secure the mirror in the channel frame.

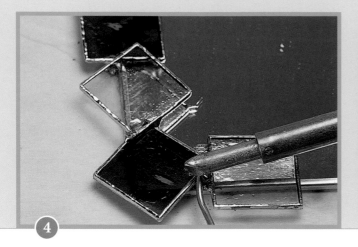

4

5

Attach glass to mirror

Using the pattern as a guide, lay the glass pieces around the mirror, positioning them on top of the zinc channel. There must be a point of contact between each square and either the channel or the tinned edges of an adjoining piece of glass (or both). Working along the perimeter, brush flux only at the contact points. Be conservative with the application, as flux can damage the mirror. To avoid breaking the mirror, reduce the heat on the soldering iron to 80°F (27°C). Then, secure the glass pieces to the frame or to the adjoining piece by letting a drop or two of solder fall on each point of contact. As you apply the glass pieces, keep in mind that the four corner pieces should be applied symmetrically.

Add decorative soldering

Drop a few extra beads of solder along the edges of each square for a decorative touch (see *Tip* below).

TIP
Decorative bead soldering can make any stained glass object more interesting. After fully soldering all the seams, you can add ornamental touches with additional soldering. First, reduce the heat of the soldering iron to about 80°F (27°C). Hold the soldering iron slightly above the seam or edge, then drop the solder, allowing it to form single beads along the soldered surface. Add beading until you achieve the desired decorative effect.

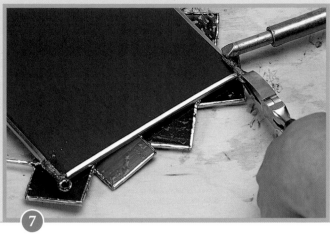

Tin hangers

Brush the brass hangers with flux, then tin the hangers to make them the same color as the soldered areas.

Attach hangers

Turn the piece over. Lay the tinned hangers along the zinc channel at the two upper corners, with only the hook extending above the top edge. Holding the hook in place with grozing pliers, brush flux sparingly onto the hangers and the corners, then solder the hanger to the channel. Make sure that the hangers are secure, reinforcing with a bit more flux and solder as necessary. Clean the glass with soapy water to remove any flux, then dry with a soft cloth. If desired, apply patina, following the package instructions. Clean again with warm, soapy water, then dry.

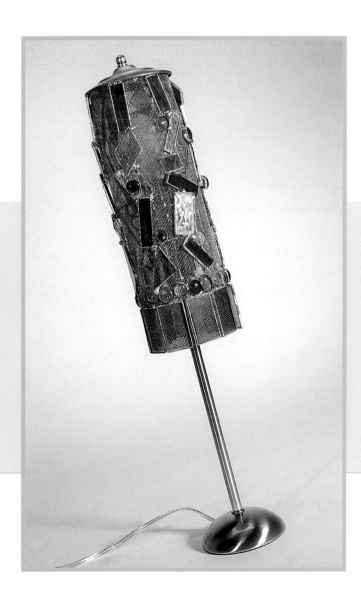

ANOTHER IDEA
Once you have become familiar with stained glass techniques, you'll discover a world of exciting possibilities. Be imaginative— design your own template to construct a one-of-a-kind creation, such as this lampshade.

Dragonfly
Garden Stake

The stained glass master Louis Comfort Tiffany used green and gold dragonflies as a motif on his signature lampshades. It is easy to understand why. After all, what could be a more suitable medium than stained glass to capture the iridescent wings and buzzing energy of these beautiful creatures?

Now it's your turn to create an updated version of stained glass dragonflies. Attached to a stake, your zigzagging insects are free to return to their natural outdoor environment. Use the dragonfly stake as a garden accessory during the warm months, then bring it inside during the winter to dress up your houseplants or add height to a favorite arrangement. This is one breed of insects that you will enjoy having around throughout the year!

TOOLS AND MATERIALS

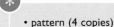

- pattern (4 copies)
- wooden work surface
- household scissors
- copper foil shears
- glass: violet iridized ripple, caramel opalescent streaky, reddish purple cathedral, bluish purple cathedral, root beer cathedral, gold water (refer to pattern for sizes)
- 2 glass nuggets: purple cathedral, gold iridized

- spray adhesive
- low-tack or masking tape
- marker
- pistol-grip glass cutter
- grozing pliers
- running pliers
- electric glass grinder
- copper foil, regular and wave
- pen, pencil or marker

- T-square
- flux brush
- liquid flux
- solder
- soldering iron, with iron station and temperature control
- copper screen
- soapy water and soft cloth
- 3' (1m) zinc H-channel, 3/8"–1/2" (10–13mm) width

Preparation

Cut two copies of the pattern apart with household scissors and copper foil shears, spray the glass with adhesive, then affix the individual pattern pieces to the appropriate colored glass. Score the glass along the edges of the adhered paper and break the glass at the score line. Use a glass grinder to smooth out the edges of the glass pieces. Soak the pieces in warm water and remove the paper, then label each piece with its corresponding number, using low-tack tape and a marker. For a more detailed explanation, see *Basic Techniques*, pages 12–17.

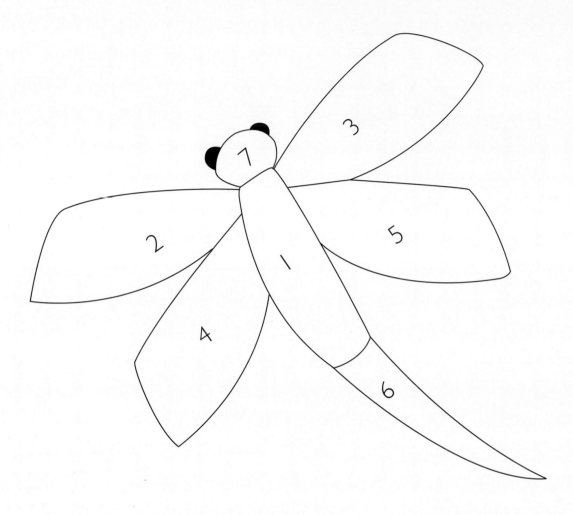

DRAGONFLY PATTERN

Enlarge this pattern by 133% using a photocopier. Make four copies, two for the first dragonfly and two for the second. Label one set of copies as Dragonfly 1 and the other set as Dragonfly 2.

Color Key

Use this key to select your glass, or choose your own palette instead. Listed below are the glass colors used in the project, followed by the corresponding pattern piece numbers.

Dragonfly 1
- *violet iridized ripple: 2, 3*
- *caramel opalescent streaky: 4, 5*
- *reddish purple cathedral: 1*
- *bluish purple cathedral: 6*
- *purple cathedral nugget: 7*

Dragonfly 2
- *caramel opalescent streaky: 2, 3*
- *violet iridized ripple: 4, 5*
- *root beer cathedral: 1*
- *gold water: 6*
- *gold iridized nugget: 7*

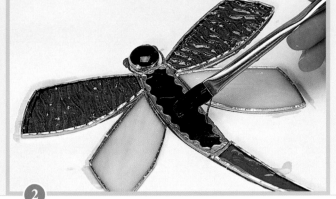

Prepare glass and wrap pieces for Dragonfly 1

Cut, grind and label all glass. Wrap each piece of glass for Dragonfly 1 with copper foil, using wave foil to wrap the body piece (piece 1). With the side of a pen, pencil or marker, burnish the copper foil.

Apply flux

Position the glass pieces on top of the pattern so that all pieces fit together tightly. With a flux brush, apply flux to all copper foil areas.

TIP

A variation of the standard adhesive-backed copper foil, wave foil features a decorative zigzag edge. When solder is applied, it follows the wave design, creating ornamental edging and adding interest to your stained glass piece.

Solder

Tack solder the joints to keep the glass pieces in place, then tin the edges of the piece so that there is no copper showing. Bead solder all the seams.

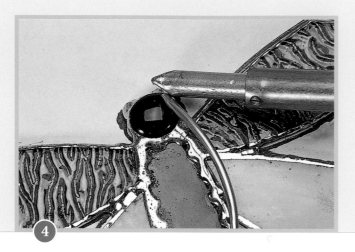

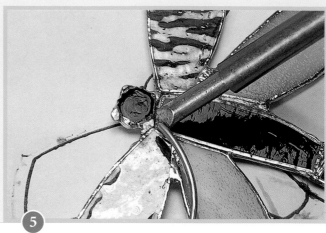

Add eyes

Add eyes to the dragonfly head by dropping a bit of solder onto the tinned edge of each side of the head nugget.

Solder reverse side

Turn the piece over and tin any edges that need to be touched up. Flat solder the seams on the back side. Add extra solder around the nugget to secure the head.

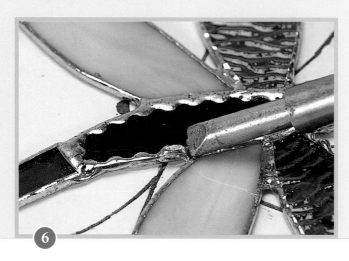

Correct imperfections

Turn the piece back over to the front. Check the front for any imperfections. If necessary, touch up using the solder and soldering iron to smooth out any bumps or melt-throughs. (See *Tip* at right for more information about correcting imperfections.)

TIP

Imperfections are common in any soldering job—the good news is that they are easy to repair! A "melt-through" occurs when solder is too hot and melts through the seam, creating a blob of solder on the reverse side. You can correct a melt-through by using the solder and soldering iron to melt the blob of solder and spread it out evenly onto the adjoining seams. Any remaining imperfections along the soldered seams can be smoothed out in the same manner.

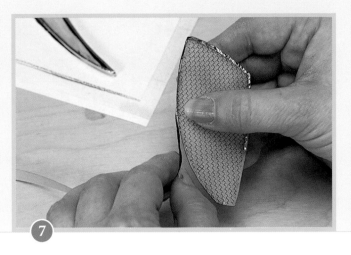

Wrap pieces for Dragonfly 2

Begin wrapping copper foil around the glass for Dragonfly 2 as you did for the first. Before wrapping the two upper wings, cut two pieces of copper screen to the size of each wing. Lay the copper screen over the glass surface, then wrap with copper foil as normal, securing the screen to the glass by folding the foil over the mesh.

Solder

Brush flux onto all the copper foil areas. Tack solder the pieces in place, then tin the edges. Be sure to completely tin the areas where the copper screen and the copper foil meet. Bead solder the front seams and flat solder the back seams until there is no copper showing, as you did with Dragonfly 1. Add drops of solder to the nugget to create eyes. To bring out the texture of the screen overlay, let the solder spread slightly from the edges into the screen.

Correct imperfections

Check the piece for any imperfections. If necessary, use the solder and soldering iron to smooth out any bumps or melt-throughs.

Attach dragonflies to zinc channel

Wash the two dragonflies with soapy water and dry with a soft cloth. Lay both dragonflies along the top of the zinc H-channel. Apply flux to all points of contact between the soldered areas and the channel, then secure the pieces to the channel by soldering at each contact point. Turn the stake over, and secure the back in the same manner. Use a damp cloth and soapy water to wash away any remaining flux, then dry.

Bird-of-Paradise Window

While this panel echoes the traditional beauty of aged stained glass windows, its striking design, based on the exotic bird-of-paradise flower, has a contemporary flair. So, whether your style is antique or modern, or somewhere between the two, this dramatic design makes a beautiful addition to any room.

As you begin the project, consider how a variety of glass types can be incorporated into the design. Be creative in using different colors and textures to represent the flower petals, the leaves and even the border. For the bird-of-paradise blossom, choose mottled or streaky red and orange glass that includes variations of white, yellow and pink. This kind of variation adds interest, depth and eye-catching contrast.

TOOLS AND MATERIALS

- pattern (2 copies)
- wooden work surface
- household scissors
- copper foil shears
- glass: red muffle, reddish orange cathedral, orange mottled, green mottled, cobalt blue cathedral, violet opalescent, pink opalescent (refer to pattern for sizes)
- spray adhesive
- low-tack or masking tape
- marker

- pistol-grip glass cutter
- grozing pliers
- running pliers
- electric glass grinder
- copper foil
- pen, pencil or marker
- T-square
- flux brush
- liquid flux
- solder

- soldering iron, with iron station and temperature control
- 5' (1.5m) zinc U-channel, 3/8" (10mm) width
- hand saw
- miter box
- horseshoe nails
- hammer
- wire brush (optional)
- 2 brass hangers
- soapy water and soft cloth
- patina

Preparation

Cut a copy of the pattern apart with household scissors and copper foil shears, spray the glass with adhesive, then affix the individual pattern pieces to the appropriate colored glass. Score the glass along the edges of the adhered paper and break the glass at the score line. Use a glass grinder to smooth out the edges of the glass pieces. Soak the pieces in warm water and remove the paper, then label each piece with its corresponding number, using low-tack tape and a marker. For a more detailed explanation, see *Basic Techniques*, pages 12–17.

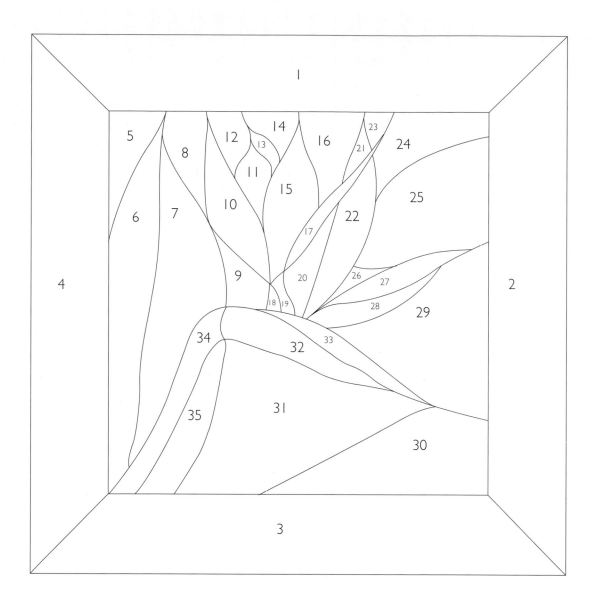

BIRD-OF-PARADISE PATTERN

Enlarge this pattern by 250% using a photocopier. Make two copies. (Some photocopiers only enlarge up to 200%. If this is the case, make a copy of the pattern at 200%, then photocopy that copy at 125%.)

Color Key

Use this key to select your glass, or choose your own palette instead. Listed below are the glass colors used in the project, followed by the corresponding pattern piece numbers.

- *red muffle: 1, 2, 3, 4*

- *reddish orange cathedral: 10, 15, 33*

- *orange mottled: 11, 13, 18, 19, 20, 21, 22*

- *green mottled: 6, 7, 30, 35*

- *cobalt blue cathedral: 5, 8, 9, 12, 14, 16, 23, 24, 25, 26, 29, 31*

- *violet opalescent: 17, 27, 28*

- *pink opalescent: 32, 34*

Prepare glass

Cut, grind and label the glass. Wrap each piece of glass with copper foil, then burnish the foil using the side of a pen, pencil or marker.

Position glass and apply flux

Place the pieces on top of the pattern, using a T-square to line up the outside edges at right angles. Once the perimeter is aligned with the pattern, fit the interior pieces together as tightly as possible. Brush flux onto all copper foil areas.

Tack solder

Tack solder the pieces of glass together at random points along the copper foil seams until all pieces are joined.

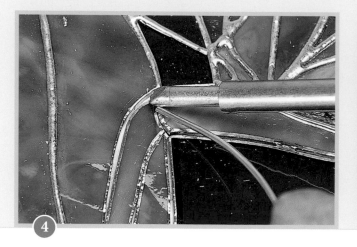

Solder

Starting at the top left, bead solder along all the copper foil seams. To allow room for the frame, stop soldering ¼" (6mm) from the outside edge.

Solder reverse side

Turn the piece over and brush flux onto the copper foil areas. Flat solder the seams on the back side. Turn the piece over to the front side and check for any imperfections. If necessary, use the solder and soldering iron to smooth out any bumps or melt-throughs.

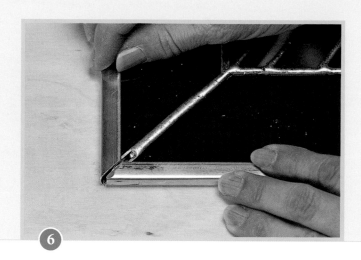

Cut and fit frame

Using a hand saw and miter box, cut four lengths of zinc U-channel to fit around each side of the glass. Finish the ends of each length at a 45° angle. Fit the channel onto the glass.

Brace frame with horseshoe nails

Gently hammer horseshoe nails into the wooden work surface to hold the zinc channel flush against the glass.

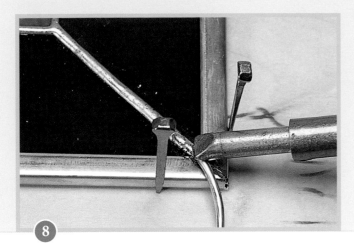

8

Secure glass in frame

Brush flux onto the corners of the zinc frame (see *Tip* below). Secure the glass in the frame by soldering the zinc corner joints. With the soldering iron, pull the solder from the stained glass seams into the solder of the corner joints. Turn the piece over, apply flux to the frame corners, then solder the seams and joints together on the back side.

9

Attach hangers

Brush the brass hangers with flux, then tin the hangers to make them the same color as the soldered surfaces. With the back side facing up, lay the hangers along the frame at the two upper corners so that only the hook extends beyond the top edge. (Alternatively, to make the hooks less noticeable, the hangers can be attached along the two top 45° angle joints of the zinc frame.) Holding the hook with grozing pliers, brush flux onto the hangers and the corners, then solder a hanger to each corner. Wash the glass with soapy water to remove any flux, then dry with a soft cloth. Patina the frame and all soldered areas, following the package instructions. Clean again with warm, soapy water, then dry.

Holiday Ornaments

All four of these festive ornaments will add sparkle to your holiday season! Display them on a window and they become marvelous sun-catchers, filtering warm winter sunlight into your home. Suspended from a branch, they make your holiday tree extra special. For a unique alternative to a decorative bow, attach one to a wrapped present—what better gift could you offer a loved one than a handmade work of art?

While these ornaments offer seasonal charm, they aren't for holiday use only. Looking for a gift idea or home decoration that can be used throughout the year? All four of these stained glass designs are versatile enough to function as year-round ornaments. Simply modify the project to suit your needs by changing the color of glass or adapting the pattern template.

TOOLS AND MATERIALS

- pattern (multiple copies, as indicated for each)
- wooden work surface
- ceramic tile (optional)
- household scissors
- copper foil shears
- glass: red cathedral, green streaky, white iridized opalescent, turquoise cathedral (refer to patterns for sizes)

- glass nuggets: 4–6 small red cathedral, 1 large clear cathedral, 1 small gold cathedral or iridized, 3 small blue or turquoise cathedral
- spray adhesive
- low-tack or masking tape
- marker
- pistol-grip glass cutter
- grozing pliers
- running pliers
- electric glass grinder

- copper foil
- pen, pencil or marker
- flux brush
- liquid flux
- solder
- soldering iron, with iron station and temperature control
- 14-gauge tinned wire
- wire cutters
- soapy water and soft cloth

Preparation

Cut a copy of the pattern apart with household scissors and copper foil shears, spray the glass with adhesive, then affix the individual pattern pieces to the appropriate colored glass. Score the glass along the edges of the adhered paper and break the glass at the score line. Use a glass grinder to smooth out the edges of the glass pieces. Soak the pieces in warm water and remove the paper, then label each piece with its corresponding number, using low-tack tape and a marker. For a more detailed explanation, see *Basic Techniques*, pages 12–17.

Ringing Bell

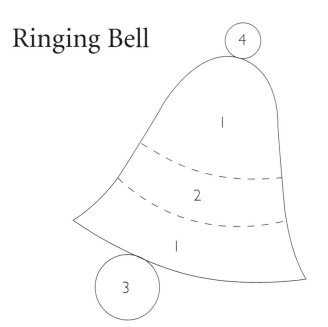

CHRISTMAS BELL PATTERN
Enlarge this pattern by 222% using a photocopier. (Some photo-copiers only enlarge up to 200%. If this is the case, make a copy of the pattern at 200%, then photocopy that copy at 111%.) Make three copies, one as a template for cutting the entire bell (piece 1), one as a template for cutting the decorative band (piece 2), and one as a template for assembling the ornament.

Color Key

Use this key to select your glass, or choose your own palette instead. Listed at right are the glass colors used in the project, followed by the corresponding pattern piece numbers.

- **red cathedral:** 1 *(note that this piece is the entire bell shape; piece 2 will be placed directly on top of piece 1)*
- **green streaky:** 2
- **large clear nugget:** 3
- **small red cathedral nugget:** 4

Prepare glass

Cut, grind and label the glass. Wrap each piece of glass, including the glass nuggets, with copper foil. Burnish the foil using the side of a pen, pencil or marker.

Apply flux

Lay the glass pieces out on your work surface. With a flux brush, apply flux to all copper foil areas.

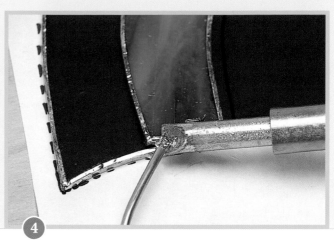

Tin copper foil edges

On a ceramic tile, tin all the copper foil surfaces of the glass pieces, including the glass nuggets. (See *Tip* below for more information about tinning on a ceramic tile.)

Solder

Position the glass pieces on top of the pattern. Place the green band of glass (piece 2) on top of the red glass (piece 1), as indicated by the pattern. Brush flux along the coinciding edges where the two pieces meet, then secure the pieces together by flat soldering.

Attach red nugget

Apply a bit of flux, then solder the red nugget to the top of the bell, securing the two pieces together by dropping solder where the two pieces meet.

TIP

When tinning small pieces of glass such as nuggets, use the length of the solder to rotate the object until you've covered all the copper foil areas. Glass rotates easily on a piece of ceramic tile, making it an ideal surface for tinning small objects.

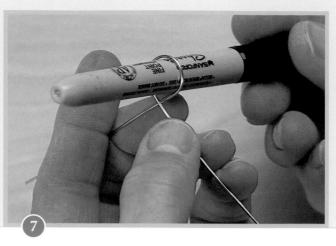

Attach clear nugget

Apply a bit of flux, then solder the clear nugget to the bottom left of the bell, securing the two pieces together by dropping solder where the pieces meet.

Create hanger

Curl a piece of wire around a marker, making a loop about 1" (3cm) long, then twisting the ends a few times to secure the loop. Fashion each end of the wire into a crook to fit along the perimeter of the red nugget. Trim any excess ends with wire cutters.

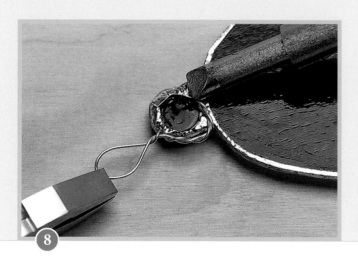

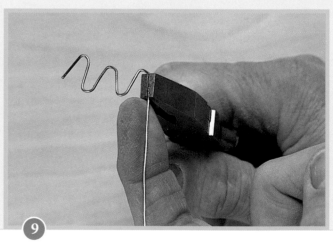

Attach hanger

Turn the piece over. Place the hanger over the back of the red nugget so that the wire ends follow along the soldered edge. Brush flux on the wire and around the tinned nugget. Holding the wire in place with grozing pliers, secure the wire to the piece by soldering along the red nugget.

Crimp wire

Place one end of an 8" (20cm) length of wire between the jaws of the grozing pliers. While gripping the wire, bend the remaining length around the outside edge of one plier jaw. Repeat this crimping technique until you have a length of accordion-shaped wire that will fit all the way across the green band of glass.

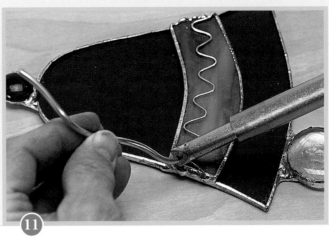

Attach crimped wire

Using wire cutters, trim the accordion wire to the length of the green band of glass. Brush on a bit of flux, then solder both ends of the wire to the tinned edge of the green glass.

Add decorative soldering

Add some decorative soldering by dropping three beads of solder along each end of the green glass. To do so, hold the iron slightly above the piece so that the solder will cool slightly and form a bead as it drops on the tinned edge. This is a decorative touch, but it also helps to hold the accordion wire in place. Wash the piece with soapy water to remove the flux and dry with a soft cloth.

RINGING BELL

You can use colors other than red and green to create a simple variation. White opalescent glass, combined with other soft colors, will transform this piece into a ringing wedding bell—the perfect gift for a newlywed couple.

Holiday Tree

3

I

2

HOLIDAY TREE PATTERN
Enlarge this pattern by 125% using a photocopier. Make two copies.

Color Key
Use this key to select your glass, or choose your own palette instead. Listed at right are the glass colors used in the project, followed by the corresponding pattern piece numbers.

- *green streaky: I*
- *red cathedral: 2*
- *small gold cathedral or iridized nugget: 3*
- *small red cathedral nuggets: on tree*

Prepare glass

Cut, grind and label the glass. Wrap each piece of glass, including the glass nuggets, with copper foil. Burnish the foil using the side of a pen, pencil or marker.

Tin edges

Place the glass pieces on a ceramic tile and brush the edges with flux. Tin all the copper foil surfaces.

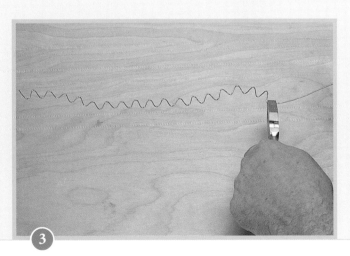

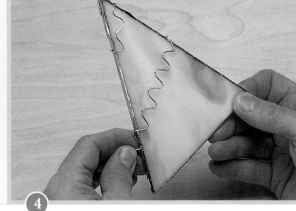

Create garland

With grozing pliers, crimp a 25" (64cm) length of tinned wire accordion-style (for further instruction, see *Ringing Bell*, step 9, page 48). Continue until you have approximately 15" (38cm) of crimped wire.

Attach garland

Turn the triangular piece of glass over so that the smoother side is facedown. Apply a bit of flux, then solder one end of the crimped wire to the top of the tree. Once the wire is secure, wrap it around at an angle to the front of the piece.

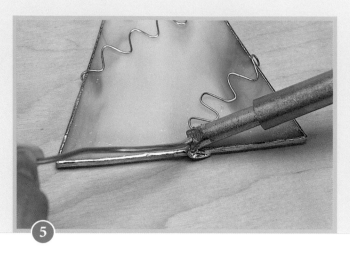

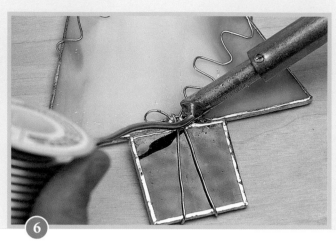

Wrap garland around tree and secure

Continue wrapping the wire around the tree like a garland, keeping the angle consistent. Trim the wire with wire cutters when you reach the bottom of the tree. Apply flux, then solder the end of the wire to the bottom of the tree.

Create gift package and attach

Transform the square piece of glass into a gift package by adding ribbon and a bow. To do so, wrap an 8" (20cm) length of wire around the square, starting in the back at the upper center. Wrap the wire down the back at a slight angle, then bring the wire up and around the front, following the same angle. Repeat to create a symmetrical ribbon. Twist the two ends of the wire together at the top, then bend the ends into the shape of a bow. Secure the wire by soldering it to the tinned edges. Trim the excess tails of the bow with wire cutters. Position the gift at the bottom of the tree in place of the trunk, then apply flux and solder along the coinciding edges where the two pieces meet. Solder the front and the back.

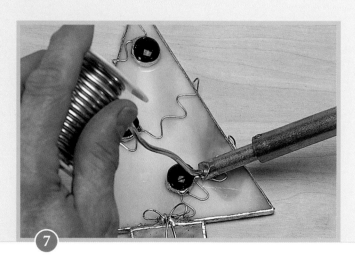

Attach nuggets

Place three red nuggets on the tree so that they touch the wire and/or a tinned edge of the glass piece. Brush the contact points with flux, then secure the nuggets in place, soldering each one to the wire and/or the edge of the glass piece.

8

Attach tree topper

Brush the tip of the tree with flux and place the gold nugget at the tip of the tree. Solder the nugget to the tree.

9

Create and attach hanger

Make a hanger from a length of wire and solder it onto the back along the tinned edges of the tree apex (for further instruction, see *Ringing Bell*, steps 7–8, page 48). Wash the piece with soapy water to remove the flux and dry with a soft cloth.

HOLIDAY TREE

You can change this Christmas tree into a beautiful natural pine by using more earthy colors and replacing the gift package with a tree trunk. Create an entire forest of pine trees for an outdoorsy, nature-loving friend.

Dove of Peace

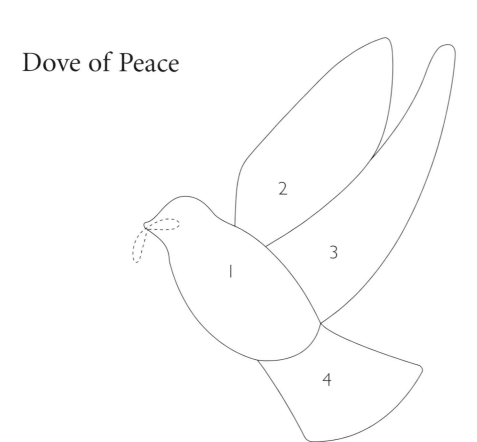

DOVE OF PEACE PATTERN
Enlarge this pattern by 180% using a photocopier. Make two copies.

Color Key
All of the glass pieces in this project are white iridized opalescent.

Prepare glass
Cut, grind and label the glass. Wrap each piece of glass with copper foil. Burnish the copper foil with the side of a pen, pencil or marker.

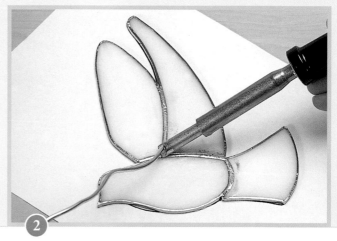

Apply flux and solder
Position the glass pieces on top of the pattern. Brush flux onto all the copper foil areas except the perimeter edges. Tack solder the pieces together, then bead solder just the interior seams.

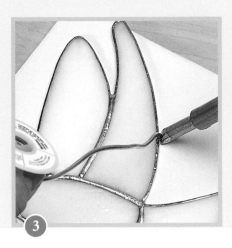

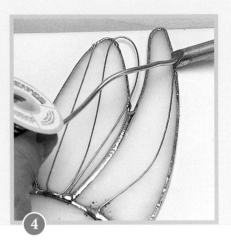

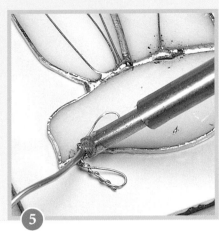

Tin edges

Place the piece on a ceramic tile and brush the perimeter edges with flux. Tin the edges of the piece.

Add decorative wire

Place one end of an 18" (46cm) length of wire at the top of the left wing, apply flux, then tack solder it to the edge. Run the wire down to the bottom of the wing, up to the top, and back down to the bottom, applying flux and tack soldering it at each turn. Trim the excess and solder the end to the wing's bottom seam. Place the end of an 8" (20cm) length of wire at the bottom center of the right wing, apply flux, then solder it to the wing's bottom seam. Run the wire up to the top of the right wing, apply flux, tack solder, then trim.

Add olive branch

Cut a 4" (10cm) length of wire. Shape the wire into a figure-eight, making two narrow loops in the wire and twisting in the center. Brush the dove's beak with flux and solder the olive branch in place.

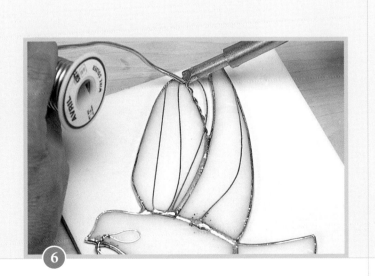

Add decorative soldering and attach hanger

Drop decorative beads of solder along the right edge of the left wing. Make a hanger from a length of wire and solder it onto the back between the wing and the head (for further instruction, see *Ringing Bell*, steps 7–8, page 48). Wash the piece with soapy water to remove the flux and dry with a soft cloth.

DOVE OF PEACE

The dove is a perfect emblem of peace and friendship, no matter what the season.

55

Winter Snowflake

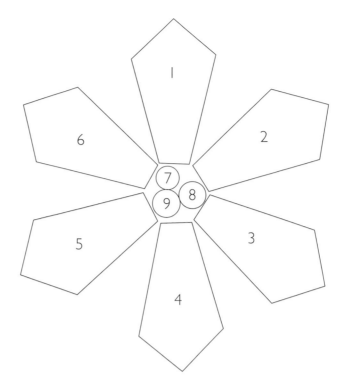

WINTER SNOWFLAKE PATTERN
Enlarge this pattern by 200% using a photocopier. Make two copies.

Color Key

Use this key to select your glass, or choose your own palette instead. Listed at right are the glass colors used in the project, followed by the corresponding pattern piece numbers.

- *turquoise cathedral:* 1, 2, 3, 4, 5, 6
- *small blue or turquoise cathedral nuggets:* 7, 8, 9

1

Prepare glass

Cut, grind and label the glass. Wrap each piece of glass, including the nuggets, with copper foil. Burnish the copper foil using the side of a pen, pencil or marker.

2

Apply flux, tack solder and tin edges

Position the pieces on top of the pattern. Brush flux onto all copper foiled areas. Tack solder the snowflake arms together at each joint. Tin all the edges of the piece, including the edges of the interior hexagonal opening.

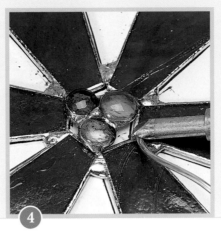

3

Join nuggets
Place the three glass nuggets in a triangular-shaped cluster and brush with flux. Drop solder into the center of the nuggets to secure the three pieces together. Tin the edges of the nugget cluster. Turn the cluster over, apply flux and reinforce with drops of solder in the center.

4

Secure nugget cluster to body
Place the nugget cluster on top of the interior hexagonal opening, making sure that the tinned outer edges of the nuggets touch the soldered joints of the snowflake. Apply flux and solder the cluster to the main piece at all points of contact. Reinforce the joints by building up solder in the opening between each snowflake arm.

5

Reinforce back
Turn the piece over and brush with flux. Tin all the edges of the back side. Further secure the nugget cluster from the back by soldering it at all points of contact with the main piece.

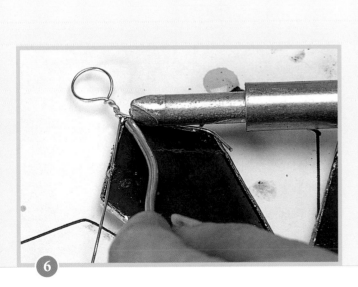

6

Create hanger
Make a hanger from a length of wire and solder it onto the back along the top tinned edges of one snowflake arm (for further instruction, see *Ringing Bell*, steps 7–8, page 48). Wash the piece with soapy water to remove the flux and dry with a soft cloth.

✳

WINTER SNOWFLAKE
Change the color of the snowflake and it becomes a beautiful geometric design, appropriate at any time of the year.

Hanging
Picture Frame

Insert a favorite photograph into this hanging frame and you've created a personal treasure! Every year, we add our best family portrait to our collection and display the photo frames up and down the staircase railing. A fireplace mantel would also be an ideal display area. Before you know it, you too will have an entire collection of framed memories!

The beveled glass is a nice touch, giving the frame a customized, finished look. You can order a piece of beveled glass cut to size at most glass stores or stained glass shops. To tailor this frame to your taste, replace the white opalescent background glass with a different color.

TOOLS AND MATERIALS

* pattern (1 copy)
* wooden work surface
* household scissors
* glass: clear beveled, white opalescent; each piece cut to 4" x 4" (10cm x 10cm)
* spray adhesive
* low-tack or masking tape
* marker
* pistol-grip glass cutter
* grozing pliers

* running pliers
* electric glass grinder
* copper foil, regular and wave
* pen, pencil or marker
* cardboard, approximately 3" x 5" (8cm x 13cm)
* flux brush
* liquid flux
* solder
* soldering iron, with iron station and temperature control

* two small blocks of wood, approximately 3" x 3" x 5" (8cm x 8cm x 13cm)
* 4' (1.3m) 12- or 14-gauge tinned wire
* wire cutters
* soapy water and soft cloth
* colored wire
* 6 decorative glass beads with holes in center

Preparation

Cut out a copy of the pattern with household scissors, spray the glass with adhesive, then affix the individual pattern pieces to the appropriate colored glass. Score the glass along the edges of the adhered paper and break the glass at the score line. Use a glass grinder to smooth out the edges of the glass pieces. Soak the pieces in warm water and remove the paper, then label each piece with its corresponding number, using low-tack tape and a marker. For a more detailed explanation, see *Basic Techniques*, pages 12–17.

```
I
FRONT
```

```
2
BACK
```

HANGING PICTURE FRAME PATTERN

Enlarge this pattern by 143% using a photocopier. Make one copy.

Color Key

Use this key to select your glass, or choose your own palette instead. Listed below are the glass colors used in the project, followed by the corresponding pattern piece numbers.

- *clear beveled: 1*

- *white opalescent: 2*

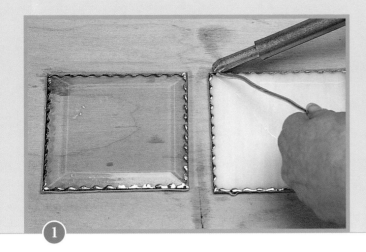

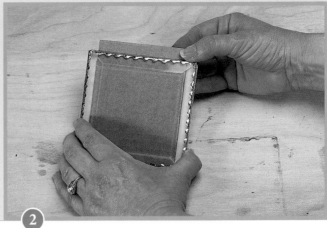

Prepare glass

Cut, grind and label the glass. (You may need to purchase a precut piece of beveled glass.) Wrap each piece of glass with wave copper foil. When applying foil to the clear glass, be sure that the wave design is on the same side as the raised bevel. Burnish the copper foil. Apply flux to the foil, then tin all copper foiled areas. With a soft, damp cloth and soapy water, thoroughly clean and dry both sides of each piece of glass.

Insert cardboard

Sandwich the piece of cardboard between the two pieces of glass, with the beveled side of the clear glass facing out. Allow one end of the cardboard to extend beyond one edge of the glass pieces; this is the top of the frame.

TIP

As you work, deposits tend to build up on the tip of your soldering iron. Keep the tip clean by periodically wiping it on the sponge included with your iron station. Alternatively, you can brush a bit of flux on the tip while it's hot to remove the deposits. You can also use a special cleaning stone, available at stained glass stores.

Seal side and bottom edges

Holding the two pieces of glass together, run copper foil around the perimeter of three sides of the glass–cardboard–glass sandwich. Do not foil the top side with the exposed cardboard. The foil should bridge the gap between the two pieces of glass. Tighten the grip of the foil seal by burnishing it with the side of a pen, pencil or marker.

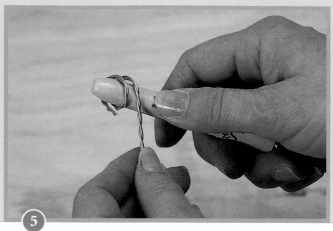

(4)

(5)

Solder top and bottom edges

Prop the glass straight up against a block of wood or brace it between two blocks of wood so that one sealed copper foil edge is face up. Brush flux onto the copper foil. Keeping the cardboard centered between the two pieces of glass, flat solder the foiled edge. Repeat with the two other foiled edges until all the copper foil has been soldered.

Create curlicue

Twist a piece (or two pieces) of tinned wire to form a 22" (56cm) length (see *Tip* below for instructions). Wrap one end of the wire twice around a marker to create a curlicue.

TIP

Here is an easy way to create decorative wire. The result is a twisted length of wire—fun, versatile and strong! Feel free to add some flair by using two or more different colored pieces of wire instead of one single piece.

First, stretch and straighten the wire. To do so, attach a lead vise to a table edge. Secure one end of a piece of wire to the vise, then take hold of the other end with a pair of pliers. Pull the wire until all the kinks are out and wire is straight. (If you do not have a vise, you can have a friend hold the end of the wire with a firm grip.)

Now, twist the wire. Replace the drill bit on an electric handheld drill with an eyelet. Take the piece of straightened wire and thread it through the eyelet. Pull both ends of the wire so that the length is even on either side of the eyelet, then attach both ends to the lead vise that has

been secured to the table. (If you do not have a vise, you can have a friend hold the two ends of the wire with a pair of pliers.) Turn the drill on, starting on low

speed and then slowly increasing speed, allowing the two ends of wire to twist together into a single length. Use wire cutters to remove the wire from the eyelet.

Form handle and secure to frame

Position the curlicue at one bottom corner of the glass. Lay the length of wire along the adjacent soldered edge. Brush flux along the edge, then secure the wire by soldering it to the top, center and bottom of the edge. Curve the wire over the top edge of the glass to form a handle, then lay the remaining wire along the other soldered side. Brush flux along the edge, then secure the wire by soldering it to the top, center and bottom of the edge.

Fasten handle on other side and finish end

Twist the remaining wire into a curlicue at the bottom corner to match the other side. Use wire cutters to trim off any leftover wire.

Thread beads

Thread three of the decorative glass beads onto colored wire. Make a loop with the wire, then pull the tail all the way back through the bead openings.

Secure beads and hang from curlicues

Twist the wire ends together to prevent the beads from slipping off, then trim off any excess wire. Slip the looped end of the bead decoration onto one curlicue so that it hangs from one corner. Repeat the process with the other three glass beads, and hang from the other corner curlicue. Remove the cardboard from the glass and replace it with a favorite photograph. Wipe the entire length of the wire handle with a damp cloth to remove any flux.

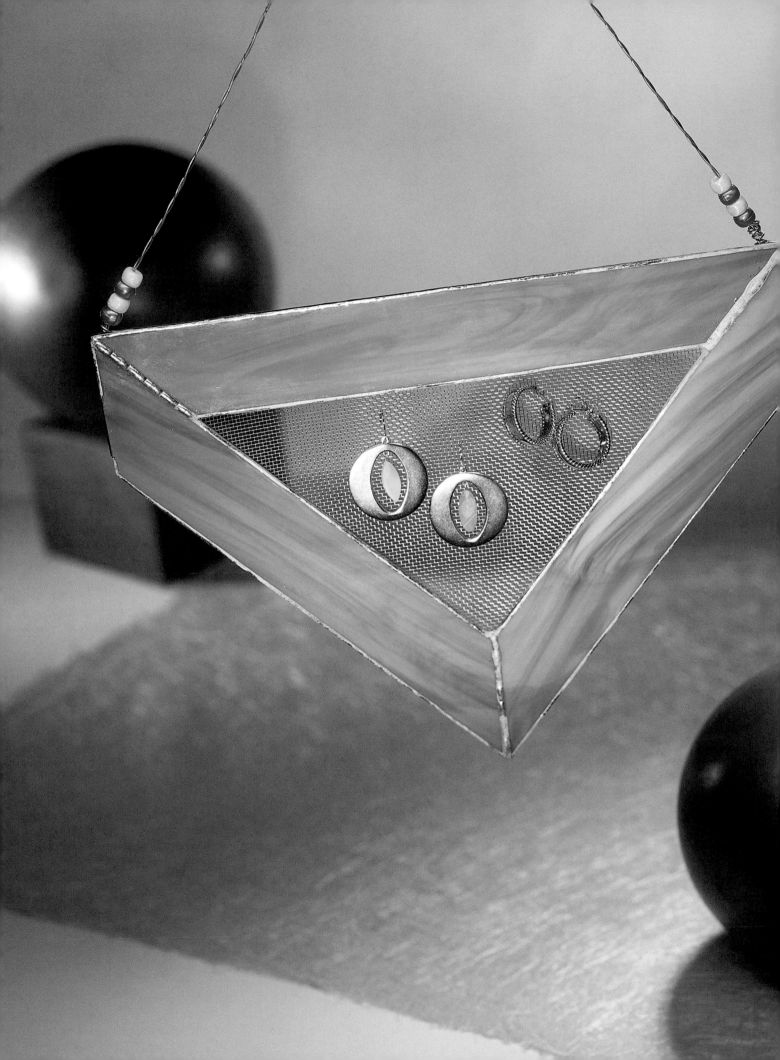

Triangular
Earring Holder

Windows and panels are not the only forms of stained glass art. Stretch your creative limits beyond traditional formats and you're bound to come up with more functional and more modern designs, such as this earring holder. These original kinds of objects are always sure to be crowd-pleasers and attention-getters!

Capable of accenting any room, this earring holder keeps your jewelry organized beautifully. Simply hook the earrings through the copper screen, and they'll always be in view and ready for your choosing. Why hide your favorite earrings away in a jewelry box when you can display them as a piece of art on the wall?

TOOLS AND MATERIALS

- pattern (2 copies)
- wooden work surface
- household scissors
- copper foil shears
- glass: turquoise streaky, bluish gray opalescent (refer to pattern for sizes)
- spray adhesive
- low-tack or masking tape
- marker
- pistol-grip glass cutter

- grozing pliers
- running pliers
- electric glass grinder
- copper foil
- pen, pencil or marker
- flux brush
- liquid flux
- solder
- soldering iron, with iron station and temperature control

- clear silicone adhesive sealant, in tube or gun
- copper screen
- 2 lengths of 12-gauge colored wire, 24" (61cm) each
- wire cutter
- 8 blue and white decorative beads with holes in center
- soapy water and soft cloth

Preparation

Cut a copy of the pattern apart with household scissors and copper foil shears, spray the glass with adhesive, then affix the individual pattern pieces to the appropriate colored glass. Score the glass along the edges of the adhered paper and break the glass at the score line. Use a glass grinder to smooth out the edges of the glass pieces. Soak the pieces in warm water and remove the paper, then label each piece with its corresponding number, using low-tack tape and a marker. For a more detailed explanation, see *Basic Techniques*, pages 12–17.

FRONT

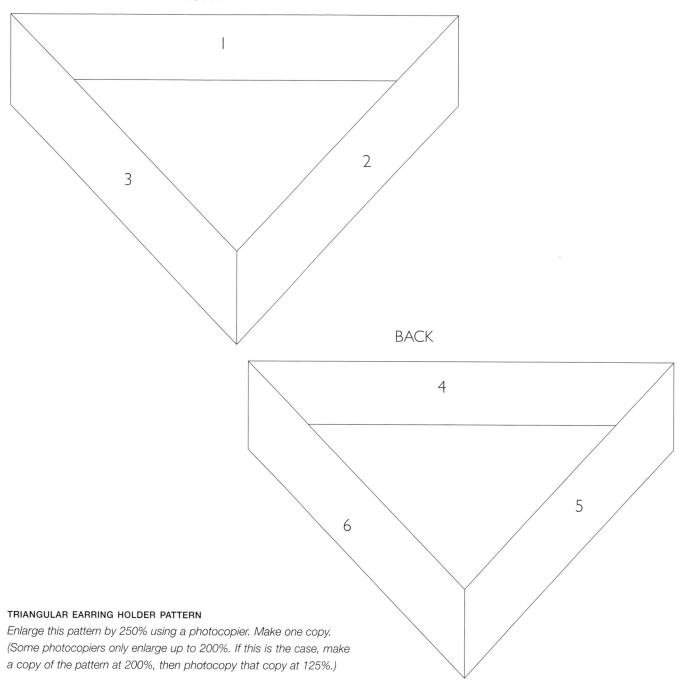

1

3   2

BACK

4

6   5

TRIANGULAR EARRING HOLDER PATTERN
Enlarge this pattern by 250% using a photocopier. Make one copy.
(Some photocopiers only enlarge up to 200%. If this is the case, make
a copy of the pattern at 200%, then photocopy that copy at 125%.)

Color Key
Use this key to select your glass, or choose
your own palette instead. Listed at right are the
glass colors used in the project, followed by the
corresponding pattern piece numbers.

• *turquoise streaky:* 1, 2, 3 *(front)*

• *bluish gray opalescent :* 4, 5, 6 *(back)*

Prepare glass

Cut, grind and label the glass. Wrap each piece of glass with copper foil. Burnish the foil using the side of a pen, pencil or marker.

Solder front piece

Position the glass pieces on top of the front pattern. With a flux brush, apply flux to all copper foil areas. Tack solder the joints and tin the edges, then flat solder the seams. Turn the piece over, apply flux, and tin the copper foil areas of the reverse side, including the seams.

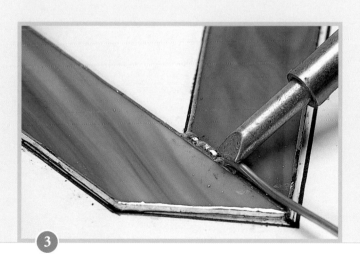

Add decorative soldering

Turn the piece back over so that it is faceup. Reduce the heat on your soldering iron to 80°F (27°C), then add decorative bead soldering to the seams. You can create a dash design by using the flat chisel tip of the iron to make repeated strokes along the seam.

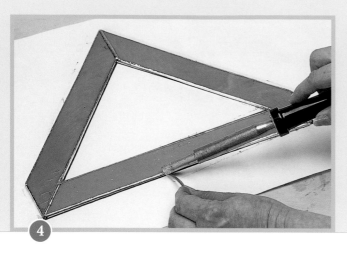

Solder back piece

Position the pieces on top of the back pattern. With a flux brush, apply flux to all the copper foil areas. Tack solder the joints, tin the edges, then flat solder the seams. Turn the piece over and repeat the process on the reverse side. Clean both pieces in soapy water and allow them to dry.

Add copper screen

Place the front piece facedown on your work surface. With scissors, cut a piece of copper screen to fit over the triangular opening, allowing the screen to overlap the inside perimeter by about 1" (3cm). Apply a line of silicone adhesive sealant about ½" (13mm) from the interior perimeter of the triangle. (See *Tip* below for more information about silicone sealant.) Lay the copper screen on top and press gently into the silicone.

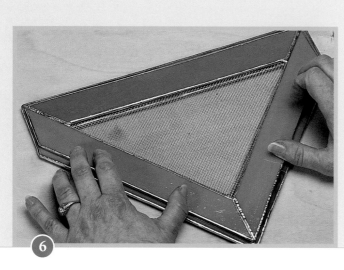

TIP
Clear silicone adhesive sealant is used to secure pieces of glass to different surfaces, including other glass pieces. Clear silicone, which can be purchased at hardware stores, is available in a tube or a gun. If you've never used silicone before, we recommend using the tube, which is a bit easier to handle.

Adhere front and back pieces

Lay the back piece on top of the copper screen, lining up the interior perimeter with that of the front piece. The exterior perimeters of the front and back pieces will not match up exactly, as the back piece is a bit smaller. Press down gently to sandwich the copper screen between the two pieces of glass. Allow the silicone to set.

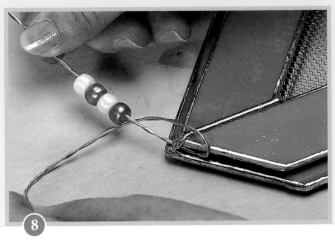

7

Solder front and back pieces together

With the back piece still facing you, brush flux onto each corner joint. Apply solder to secure the glass triangles together, drawing the solder across the corner joints to make one continuous line spanning the two pieces. Build up the bead to reinforce the the joint.

8

Slip wire through corner joint opening

Position the piece on your work surface so that the apex of the triangle is facing down. Twist the two lengths of colored wire together (for further instruction, see *Tip*, page 62). Slide four beads onto one end of the wire, alternating blue–white–blue–white. At the top left corner, slip one end of the wire between the two pieces of glass. Loop the wire through the soldered joint opening once to secure, then pull the wire through until only a few inches (several centimeters) remain on one end.

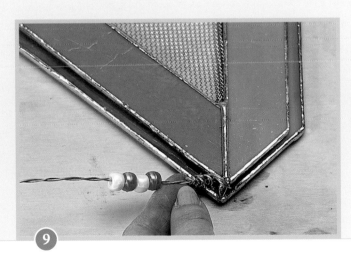

9

Form handle and secure

Twist the short end around the length of the wire to secure the beads. Curve the remaining wire across to the top right corner, forming an arched handle. Add the last four beads to the end of the wire. Again, slip the end of the wire between the two pieces of glass, then loop it through the soldered joint opening. Twist the end of the wire just below the beads to secure the wire. With a soft cloth and soapy water, wipe the entire surface of the glass and length of the wire to remove any flux, then allow the glass to dry.

Beaded
House Number

Stained glass and beads can turn something as ordinary as a house address into a work of art. With your artistic address plate prominently on display, your home will be the hit of the neighborhood! You are the designer for this piece, as you select all the elements—the numbers, the beads, the stained glass—with your home in mind.

Buy the appropriate glass numerals from a stained glass studio, then secure them with clear silicone to a contrasting background glass. The finishing touch is provided by the Bead Weaver iron wind chime frame, which features eight small holes drilled around the perimeter to accept wire and beads.

TOOLS AND MATERIALS

- pattern (1 copy)
- wooden work surface
- household scissors
- glass: caramel opalescent streaky, or color to contrast with numerals (sized to fit wind chime frame)
- spray adhesive
- pistol-grip glass cutter or circle cutter
- grozing pliers
- running pliers
- electric glass grinder

- lead channel (available at stained glass shops)
- lead nippers (available at stained glass shops)
- horseshoe nails
- hammer
- flux brush
- liquid flux
- solder
- soldering iron, with iron station and temperature control

- large address numerals
- clear silicone adhesive sealant, in tube or gun
- Kennedy/Kaleidoscope Bead Weaver iron wind chime frame
- 8' (2.5m) 14-gauge tinned wire
- wire cutters
- 20–25 decorative glass beads in several shapes and colors, with holes in center
- soapy water and soft cloth

Preparation

Cut out the pattern with household scissors, spray the glass with adhesive, then affix the pattern piece to the glass you have selected. Use a circle cutter or pistol grip glass cutter to score the glass along the edges of the adhered paper, then break the glass at the score line. Use a glass grinder to smooth out the edges of the glass. Soak the piece in warm water and remove the paper. For a more detailed explanation, see *Basic Techniques*, pages 12–17.

BEADED HOUSE NUMBER PATTERN
Enlarge this pattern by 400% using a photocopier. (Some photocopiers only enlarge up to 200%. If this is the case, make a copy of the pattern at 200%, then photocopy that copy at 200%.) Double check the size to make sure it will fit inside the wind chime frame. Make one copy.

Color Key
For the main stained glass piece, choose a color that contrasts with the numerals. If the numerals are dark, choose a light or bright color.

TIP

If your piece is exposed to the elements, check it periodically to make sure all pieces remain securely fastened in place.

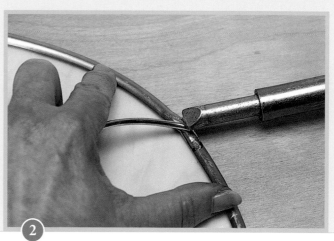

Prepare glass

Check the size of the wind chime frame. Cut the glass so that, with a lead channel around the perimeter, it will fit snugly in the frame. Grind the glass. Cut a piece of lead channel long enough to fit around the glass, using lead nippers to cut where the two ends meet. Brace the channel against the glass with horseshoe nails hammered into the wood surface, then fit the two ends together to form a joint.

Apply flux and solder

With a flux brush, apply flux to the joint. Secure the joint by soldering. Wash the joint with a soft, damp cloth to remove any flux.

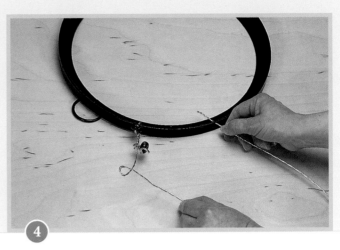

3 Attach numerals

Lay out the numerals on the glass. Apply clear silicone to the back of the numerals and adhere to the glass, attaching the center numeral(s) first, followed by the flanking numerals. Set the piece aside and allow the silicone to set.

4 Begin decorative wiring

Lay the wind chime frame facedown on the work surface. Twist two pieces of tinned wire to form a 4' (1.3m) length (for further instruction, see *Tip*, page 62). Thread the wire through one of the small holes of the frame, pulling most of the wire through to leave just a few inches (several centimeters) on one end. Add a glass bead to this short end, then secure the bead by twisting the few remaining inches (centimeters) of wire around the length.

5 Complete decorative wiring

Work the wire around the perimeter of the frame, looping it through each hole to secure it. Shape the wire with decorative twists and turns and add beads as you go along. The wire should appear as one continuous length around the border. If you use up the first length of twisted wire, create another length. Then, splice the two ends of wire together, twisting the new piece onto the existing piece. When you have finished wiring the entire perimeter, twist the end of the last wire length onto the beginning length where you started.

6 Secure glass in frame

Position the frame on the work surface so that the hanger is at the top. Apply clear silicone to the inside lip of the frame. Insert the glass into the frame and press down gently to secure it. Allow the silicone to set.

Cranberry Rose
Garden Stake

Stained glass is becoming a favorite medium for garden art, which is popping up in front and backyards everywhere! There's no better place for stained glass than the outdoors, where it captures sunlight and beautifies your garden. This cranberry rose design is fashioned from a hundred-year-old window design. Secured in an iron frame, the stained glass rose keeps its bloom when all other blossoms have disappeared.

For this project, you will be using a specially designed garden stake. The stake features an angle iron hoop frame attached to a sturdy iron rod, covered with a black powder coat to protect the iron. Displayed in this frame, any stained glass piece will be a wonderful complement to your landscape!

TOOLS AND MATERIALS

- pattern (2 copies)
- wooden work surface
- household scissors
- copper foil shears
- glass: chartreuse opalescent streaky, gray baroque, cranberry streaky (with color variation), forest green streaky, forest green water (refer to pattern for sizes)
- spray adhesive
- low-tack or masking tape

- marker
- pistol-grip glass cutter
- circle cutter (optional)
- grozing pliers
- running pliers
- electric glass grinder
- copper foil
- pen, pencil or marker
- flux brush

- liquid flux
- solder
- soldering iron, with iron station and temperature control
- soapy water and soft cloth
- Kennedy/Kaleidoscope garden stake, 12" (30cm) diameter
- clear silicone adhesive sealant, in tube or gun

Preparation

Cut a copy of the pattern apart with household scissors and copper foil shears, spray the glass with adhesive, then affix the individual pattern pieces to the appropriate colored glass. Score the glass along the edges of the adhered paper and break the glass at the score line. Use a glass grinder to smooth out the edges of the glass pieces. Soak the pieces in warm water and remove the paper, then label each piece with its corresponding number, using low-tack tape and a marker. For a more detailed explanation, see *Basic Techniques*, pages 12–17.

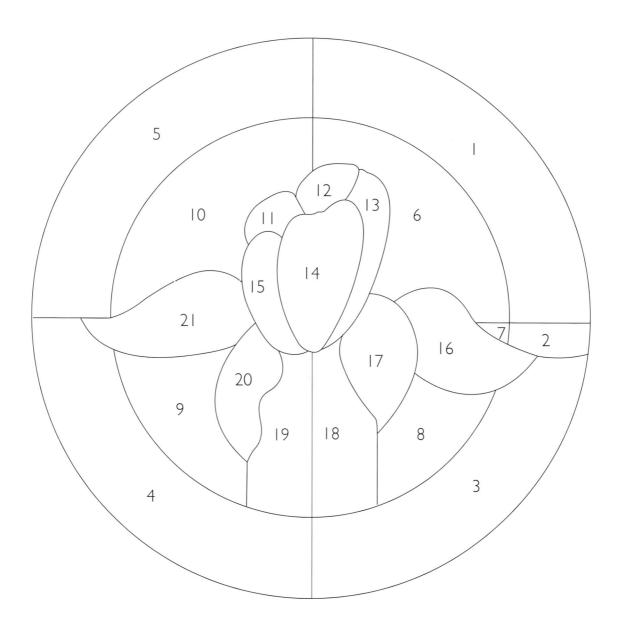

ROSE GARDEN STAKE PATTERN

Enlarge this pattern by 200% using a photocopier. Make two copies.

Color Key

Use this key to select your glass, or choose your own palette instead. Listed below and at right are the glass colors used in the project, followed by the corresponding pattern piece numbers.

- *chartreuse opalescent streaky:* 1, 2, 3, 4, 5
- *gray baroque:* 6, 7, 8, 9, 10
- *cranberry streaky (with color variation):* 11, 12, 13, 14, 15
- *forest green streaky:* 16, 17, 20, 21
- *forest green water:* 18, 19

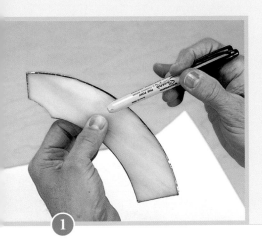

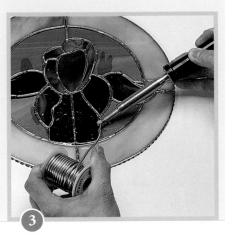

1 Prepare glass

Cut, grind and label the glass. Wrap each piece of glass with copper foil. Burnish the copper foil using the side of a pen, pencil or marker.

2 Apply flux

Position the glass pieces on top of the pattern. Make sure that all the outside pieces align with the pattern perimeter, then fit interior pieces together as tightly as possible. Brush flux onto all the copper foil areas.

3 Tack solder

Tack solder at random points along the copper foil seams until all the glass pieces are joined.

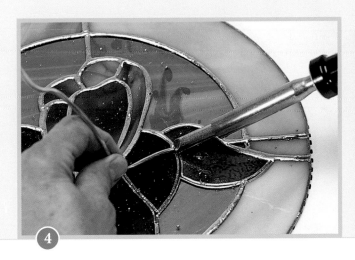

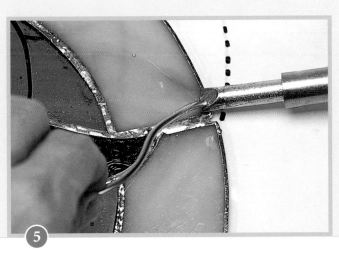

4 Solder both sides

Bead solder all the pieces of glass together along the copper foil seams, soldering continuously from one joint to the next. Turn the piece over, apply flux and flat solder the reverse side.

5 Tin edges and secure in frame

Apply flux and tin the perimeter edges so that no copper foil remains exposed. Wash the piece with soapy water to remove the flux and dry with a soft cloth. Secure the piece in the circular iron frame of the garden stake with clear silicone.

Celebration
Light Switch Plate

This light switch plate puts a new spin on stained glass art. Of course stained glass is associated with light, but light switches? Why not? Look around your home—the possibilities for stained glass projects are endless! What room wouldn't be brightened up by a touch of stained glass?

Home projects, such as this light switch plate, make perfect housewarming gifts. For new homeowners, stained glass is a unique way to make their dwelling warm and welcoming. You can be sure that your handmade gifts will be displayed with pride!

TOOLS AND MATERIALS

- pattern (2 copies)
- wooden work surface
- household scissors
- copper foil shears
- glass: spring green opaque, cobalt blue opaque (refer to pattern for sizes)
- spray adhesive
- low-tack or masking tape
- marker

- pistol-grip glass cutter
- grozing pliers
- running pliers
- electric glass grinder
- copper foil
- pen, pencil or marker
- flux brush
- liquid flux
- solder

- soldering iron, with iron station and temperature control
- 4 lengths of 22-gauge colored wire, 18" (46cm) each
- wire cutters
- soapy water and soft cloth
- 4–10 small decorative beads with holes in center
- craft glue

Preparation

Cut a copy of the pattern apart with household scissors and copper foil shears, spray the glass with adhesive, then affix the individual pattern pieces to the appropriate colored glass. Score the glass along the edges of the adhered paper and break the glass at the score line. Use a glass grinder to smooth out the edges of the glass pieces. Soak the pieces in warm water and remove the paper, then label each piece with its corresponding number, using low-tack tape and a marker. For a more detailed explanation, see *Basic Techniques*, pages 12–17.

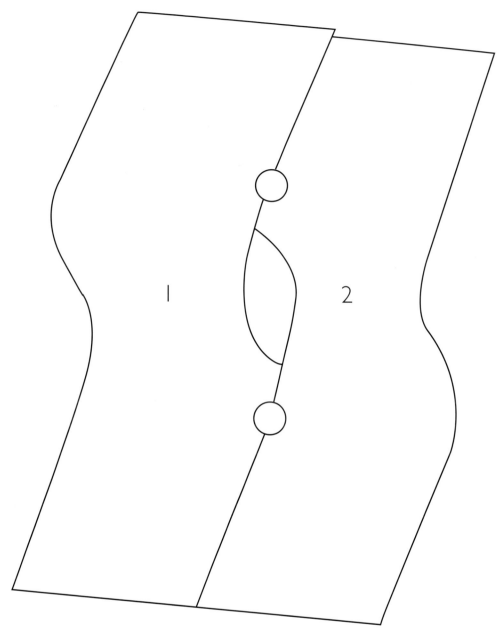

CELEBRATION LIGHT SWITCH PLATE PATTERN
Copy this pattern at 100% using a photocopier. Make two copies.

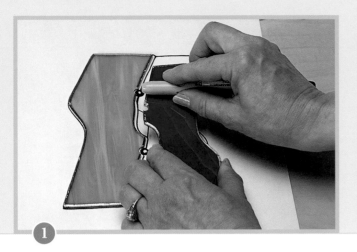

① **Prepare glass**

Cut, grind and label the glass. Wrap each piece of glass with copper foil, leaving the screw notch openings unwrapped. Burnish the copper foil using the side of a pen, pencil or marker.

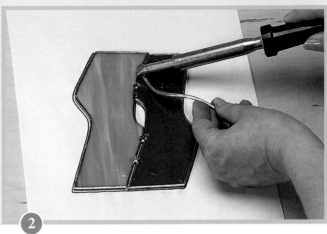

② **Apply flux and tack solder**

Place the glass pieces on top of the pattern. With a flux brush, apply flux to all copper foil areas. Join the two pieces by tack soldering at random points along the seam.

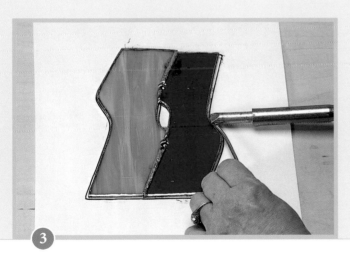

③ **Solder**

Bead solder the central seam. Tin the perimeter edges of the piece and the interior edges of the light switch opening. Turn the piece over and flat solder the seam on the reverse side. Turn the piece back over, checking for melt-throughs and correcting any imperfections.

TIP

Before cutting your glass, remove the original light switch plate that you will be replacing and compare it to the stained glass pattern. The pattern should be at least as large as the original plate but small enough to fit within the existing wall space. If necessary, adjust the pattern size to accommodate your needs.

Select opaque glass so that the light switch mechanism does not show through the plate.

Make sure to cut the screw holes large enough to accommodate screws. For precision, use a ⅛" (3mm) grinding head on the electric glass grinder to create screw notches in the glass.

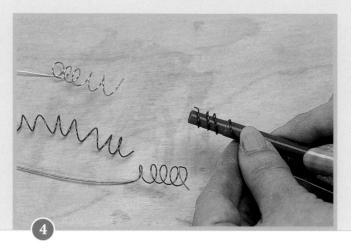

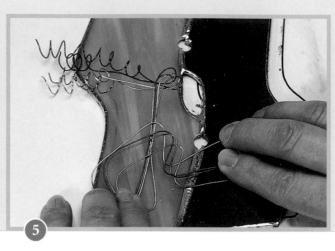

Twist wire into coils

Twist the first few inches (several centimeters) of each piece of colored wire several times around a marker to create a corkscrew effect. Leave the rest of the wire straight.

Position wire on plate

Twist the four pieces of colored wire together, making decorative bends and loops. Run the twisted wire along the left side of the plate, then bend the wire so that it crosses over the soldered seam to the right side of the plate.

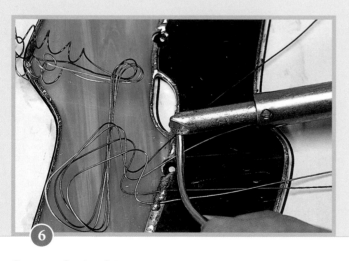

TIP

Reducing the heat on your soldering iron allows the solder to flow more smoothly, making it easier to create a bridge over the wire.

Secure wire to plate

Holding the wire down where it crosses the seam, brush flux onto the soldered area. Colored wire will not solder, so secure the wire to the light switch plate by creating a tight "bridge," stacking the solder over the wire, on top of the seam.

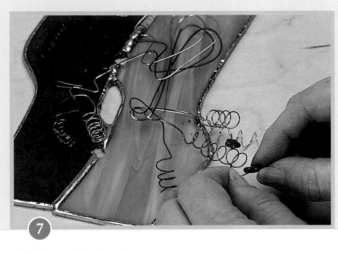

Beads are used as decorative elements in several projects. A variety of beads can be purchased from many stores, including craft and fabric stores as well as bead specialty shops. Frequently, you can find beads that complement the color and texture of the stained glass. Just make sure that the diameter of the holes in the center of the beads will accommodate the wire you are using.

7

Add decorative beads

Once the wire is secured to the plate, continue bending and twisting the wire in a decorative manner, running the wire back up along the right side of the plate. If the wire needs to be secured elsewhere on the plate, repeat the bridging process over the soldered seam. For a finishing touch, add small decorative beads to the coiled ends of the wire with touches of craft glue to hold the beads in place. Use a soft, damp cloth to remove any flux from the wire and the glass surface.

ANOTHER IDEA

Do you need to cover a double light switch? Simply adapt the template to fit your light switch and personalize it by adding your own design elements. Fun shapes and colors make a perfect accent for a child's bedroom or playroom.

Jewelry Display
Purse

An icon of modern style and femininity, the fanciful handbag has been a favorite fashion accent for generations of women. Purses of every kind, from vintage to whimsical, seem to be showing up everywhere these days—not only on boutique shelves, but in artwork, greeting cards, jewelry, papercrafts, ceramics and metalcrafts. They are the perfect accessory, whether you are dressing up an outfit, a room or a tabletop.

Unlike other conversation-piece purses, this stained glass handbag isn't just for show. It cleverly holds all your favorite jewelry along the handle. Placed on a dresser or a vanity, this purse blends fun and function with flair!

TOOLS AND MATERIALS

- pattern (multiple copies, as indicated)
- wooden work surface
- household scissors
- glass: bluish green iridized ripple, cobalt blue opaque (refer to pattern for sizes)
- spray adhesive
- low-tack or masking tape
- marker
- pistol-grip glass cutter

- grozing pliers
- running pliers
- electric glass grinder
- copper foil
- pen, pencil or marker
- flux brush
- liquid flux
- solder

- soldering iron, with iron station and temperature control
- 2 lengths of 12- or 14-gauge tinned wire, 16" (41cm) each
- ruler or straightedge
- wire cutters
- soapy water and soft cloth

Preparation

Cut out copies of the pattern pieces with household scissors, spray the glass with adhesive, then affix the individual pattern pieces to the appropriate colored glass. Score the glass along the edges of the adhered paper and break the glass at the score line. Use a glass grinder to smooth out the edges of the glass pieces. Soak the pieces in warm water and remove the paper, then label each piece with its corresponding number, using low-tack tape and a marker. For a more detailed explanation, see *Basic Techniques*, pages 12–17.

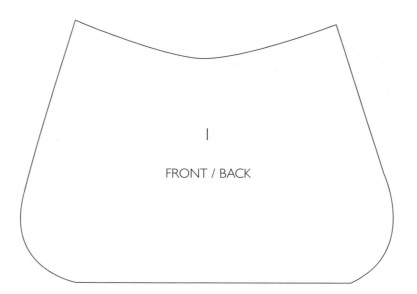

I

FRONT / BACK

3
CLASP

PURSE BODY PATTERN

Enlarge this pattern by 200% using a photocopier. Make two copies. Label one as Front and the other as Back.

PURSE CLASP PATTERN

Enlarge this pattern by 200% using a photocopier. Make one copy.

2 BOTTOM

4
HANDLE

PURSE BOTTOM PATTERN

Enlarge this pattern by 200% using a photocopier. Make one copy.

PURSE HANDLE PATTERN

Enlarge this pattern by 200% using a photocopier. Make eight copies.

Color Key

Use this key to select your glass, or choose your own palette instead. Listed below are the glass colors used in the project, followed by the corresponding pattern piece numbers.

• **bluish green iridized ripple:** I *(front)*

• **cobalt blue opaque:** I *(back),* 2 *(bottom),* 3 *(clasp),* 4 *(handle)*

Prepare glass

Cut, grind and label the glass. Wrap each piece of glass with copper foil. Burnish the foil using the side of a pen, pencil or marker.

Apply flux and tin purse body

Lay the front, back, bottom and clasp pieces on the work surface. With a flux brush, apply flux to the copper foil areas of all four pieces, then tin the copper foil surfaces. Wash the pieces with soapy water to remove any flux, then dry with a soft cloth.

Attach clasp to front piece

Lay the clasp piece vertically on the front piece, centering it from the top edge. Apply flux, then solder along the coinciding edge where the two pieces meet.

Construct purse body

Lay the bottom piece flat on the work surface. Hold the front piece up so that its bottom edge meets one long edge of the bottom piece. Shift the front piece a bit so that it stands at a slight inward angle to t he bottom piece. Holding the glass in place, brush flux along the interior seam where the edges meet. Tack solder in place, then bead solder along the seam to secure the two pieces together.

Finish constructing purse

Repeat on the other side, holding the back piece at an equal inward angle to meet the front piece. Reach inside the opening and brush flux along the interior seam where the edges meet. Tack solder in place by extending the soldering iron into the opening, then bead solder the seam together.

Secure purse corners

Brush flux at the top two corners where the front and back pieces meet. Tack solder the corners together.

Solder bottom seams

Hold the purse upside down and solder along the exterior bottom seams to secure all three pieces—front, back and bottom—together.

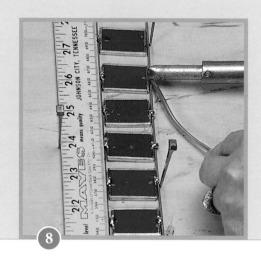

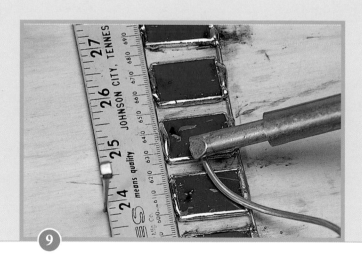

Assemble purse handle

Line up the eight remaining pieces of glass in a ladderlike formation, positioning them horizontally in a vertical row and spacing them 1/4"–3/8" (6–10mm) apart. Place one 16" (41cm) length of tinned wire on either side of the row. Brace the wire against a ruler, then anchor the wire with horseshoe nails, making sure that the glass pieces are flush against the wire. Brush flux on all points of contact between the copper foil edges of the glass and the tinned wire. Join the glass pieces to the wire by tack soldering along both sides of every piece.

Solder purse handle

Bead solder the copper foil edges to the wire, applying flux as necessary. Brush on more flux, then tin all the remaining copper foil edges. Turn the piece over and repeat the process on the reverse side, soldering and tinning the edges.

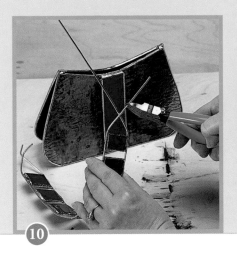

10

11

12

Finish purse handle

Turn the piece over again and, taking each end, bend it gently into an arch to form a handle. At each end, crisscross the two pieces of leftover wire. Hold the handle over the purse to determine where each side should be trimmed, then cut the wire accordingly, just beyond the crisscross.

Attach purse handle

With the handle in place, tuck a criss-crossed end inside the opening on one side. Brush flux onto the point of contact, then solder to secure the handle. Repeat on the other side.

Touch up imperfections

Examine the piece and touch up with additional soldering as necessary. Remove flux from the piece by using a soft, damp cloth to wipe the wire and the glass surface clean.

ANOTHER IDEA

Sometimes brilliant colors and swirling patterns combine to produce a piece of glass that is just too gorgeous to pass up! Select pieces of glass with unusual designs that appeal to you, then create your own template to accentuate the distinguishing features of the glass.

Bright Blue
Sunflower

Have you ever seen a blue sunflower? Maybe not in nature, but with stained glass, anything is possible! With so many beautiful variations of glass, the most striking color combination may not always be the most true to nature. Part of the joy of stained glass is using your imagination, so don't be afraid to try something a little out of the ordinary from time to time.

Patterns like these can be used to create a series of stained glass pieces. You could create one blue sunflower, one red one and one yellow one, then display all three as panels on a window or on stake frames in your garden. Wherever these sunflowers grow, they'll warm your heart through the seasons!

TOOLS AND MATERIALS

- pattern (2 copies)
- wooden work surface
- household scissors
- copper foil shears
- glass: clear water, blue streaky, variegated brown ripple (refer to pattern for sizes)
- spray adhesive
- low-tack or masking tape
- marker
- pistol-grip glass cutter

- circle cutter (optional)
- grozing pliers
- running pliers
- electric glass grinder
- copper foil
- pen, pencil or marker
- flux brush
- liquid flux
- solder

- soldering iron, with iron station and temperature control
- 4' (1.3m) zinc U-channel, 1/8" (3mm) width
- lead nippers (available at stained glass shops)
- horseshoe nails
- hammer
- 2 brass hangers
- soapy water and soft cloth
- patina (optional)
- chain or fishing line

Preparation

Cut a copy of the pattern apart with household scissors and copper foil shears, spray the glass with adhesive, then affix the individual pattern pieces to the appropriate colored glass. Score the glass along the edges of the adhered paper and break the glass at the score line. Use a glass grinder to smooth out the edges of the glass pieces. Soak the pieces in warm water and remove the paper, then label each piece with its corresponding number, using low-tack tape and a marker. For a more detailed explanation, see *Basic Techniques*, pages 12–17.

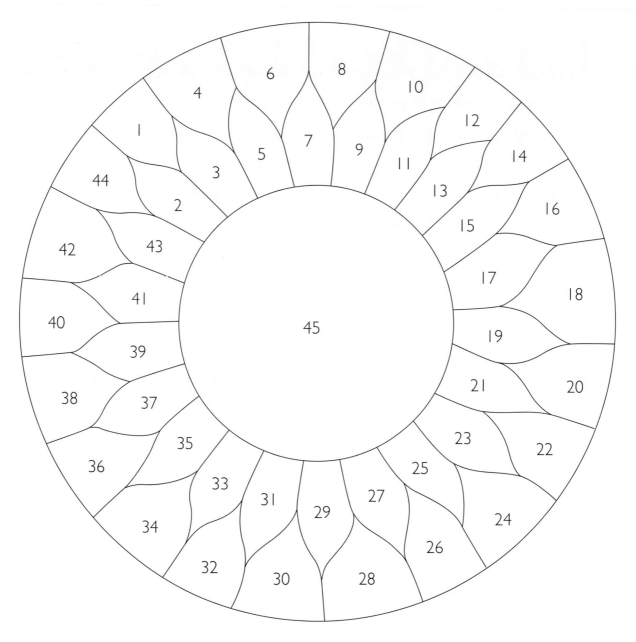

BLUE SUNFLOWER PATTERN

Enlarge this pattern by 180% using a photocopier. Make two copies.

Color Key

Use this key to select your glass, or choose your own palette instead. Listed below and at right are the glass colors used in the project, followed by the corresponding pattern piece numbers.

- *clear water:* 1, 4, 6, 8, 10, 12, 14, 16, 18, 20, 22, 24, 26, 28, 30, 32, 34, 36, 38, 40, 42, 44

- *blue streaky:* 2, 3, 5, 7, 9, 11, 13, 15, 17, 19, 21, 23, 25, 27, 29, 31, 33, 35, 37, 39, 41, 43

- *variegated brown ripple:* 45

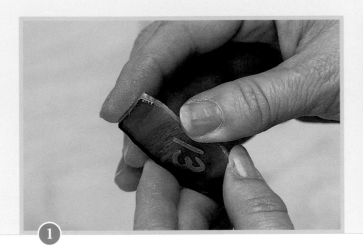

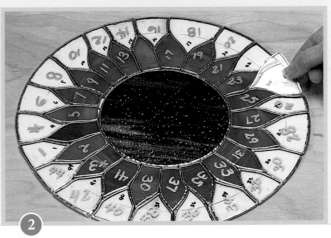

Prepare glass

Cut, grind and label the glass. Wrap each piece of glass with copper foil. Burnish the foil using the side of a pen, pencil or marker.

Position glass pieces on pattern

Position the glass pieces on top of the pattern. Make sure that all the outside pieces align with the pattern perimeter, then fit all the interior pieces together as tightly as possible.

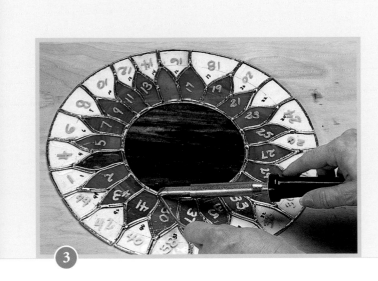

TIP

It is especially important in a stained glass object with several similarly shaped components that you carefully label all the glass pieces to correspond with the pattern. It is easy to get confused and frustrated if the pieces are not clearly and correctly identified.

Apply flux and tack solder

With a flux brush, apply flux to all copper foil areas. Tack solder the joints along the copper foil seams until all the glass pieces are secured to one another.

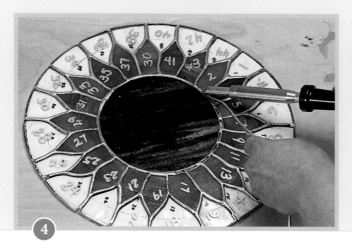

Solder front

Bead solder the pieces of glass together along the copper foil seams, beginning with the seams between all the glass petals and ending with the seam around the inner circle. To allow room for the frame, stop soldering about ⅛" (3mm) from the outside edge. Do not tin or solder around the perimeter edge.

Solder reverse side

Turn the piece over and brush flux over all the copper foil areas. Flat solder the copper foil seams on the reverse side, again leaving about a ⅛" (3mm) space from the perimeter edge. If you want to raise the bead, build up the solder by going over the seams again.

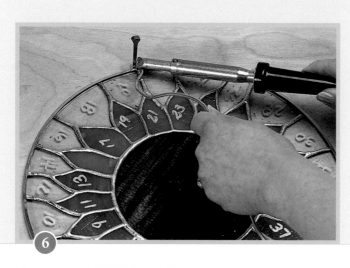

TIP

Lead nippers resemble ordinary wire cutters, but their hardened steel jaws with spring tension handles are made specifically to cut and bend lead and wire. You can purchase lead nippers at stained glass shops.

Frame glass with U-channel

Wrap the zinc U-channel around the perimeter of the piece. With lead nippers, cut the channel at the point where the two ends will meet. Position the channel ends so that they meet precisely at a soldered joint. Lay the piece flat on the work surface and use horseshoe nails to brace the channel flush against the glass until the soldering is complete.

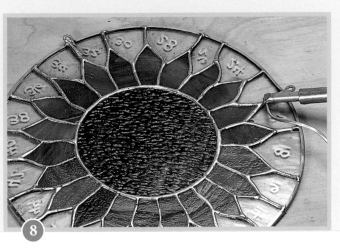

Reinforce perimeter contact ponts

Brush flux onto all perimeter points where the soldered joints meet the zinc channel. Solder each contact point to secure the glass inside the frame. Be careful when applying solder to the zinc surface, as it is difficult to correct imperfections.

Add hangers

Brush the brass hangers with flux, then tin the hangers, covering them with a thin layer of solder to match the color of the soldered joints. Turn the piece over and lay hangers at 11:00 and 1:00 positions on the circle, placing each along a soldered seam so that only the hook extends beyond the frame. Brush the contact points with flux. Secure the hangers, soldering along the seams and over the zinc channel. Clean with soapy water to remove any flux and dry with a soft cloth. If desired, apply patina to the zinc frame, following the package instructions. Clean again with warm, soapy water, then dry. To facilitate hanging, attach a chain or fishing line to the hangers.

TIP

Patina gives stained glass pieces a finished look. When applied to zinc, solder or lead, patina turns the surface black, copper or brass, depending on the kind of patina you are using. Over time, as the patina oxidizes, the soldered areas will take on a more aged appearance. To restore the original sheen of the patina, you can periodically touch up the surface with special polishing products, which are available at most stained glass stores.

In all of the projects in this book, the use of patina is optional. If you choose to use patina, purchase the kind that is made specifically for solder and lead. Always use caution when using patina; follow the instructions on the bottle, and keep it away from eyes and skin. Apply the patina with a paintbrush, then wash the piece with warm, soapy water.

Prairie Window
Nightlight

The famous American architect Frank Lloyd Wright designed not only houses but stained glass as well. Wright considered his windows, which he called "light screens," an important aspect of his architecture. He believed that the colored glass enhanced the quality of light in his structures.

Wright created the "Prairie window," a general design based on the aesthetic of the Prairie style, related to the Arts and Crafts, Craftsman and Mission styles. Wright used simple rectilinear shapes and abstract designs for these windows, and he fashioned them only as casement windows, hinged at the sides, rather than as double-hung sash windows. With straight bands of color and its wings hinged at the sides, this nightlight embodies the style of the Prairie window.

TOOLS AND MATERIALS

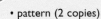

- pattern (2 copies)
- wooden work surface
- household scissors
- copper foil shears
- glass: clear beveled, cream opalescent, green opalescent, green hammered (refer to pattern for sizes)
- spray adhesive
- low-tack or masking tape

- marker
- pistol-grip glass cutter
- grozing pliers
- running pliers
- electric glass grinder
- copper foil
- pen, pencil or marker
- flux brush

- liquid flux
- small wood block or ceramic tile
- solder
- soldering iron, with iron station and temperature control
- nightlight plug (available at stained glass shops)
- soapy water and soft cloth

Preparation

Cut a copy of the pattern apart with household scissors and copper foil shears, spray the glass with adhesive, then affix the individual pattern pieces to the appropriate colored glass. Score the glass along the edges of the adhered paper and break the glass at the score line. Use a glass grinder to smooth out the edges of the glass pieces. Soak the pieces in warm water and remove the paper, then label each piece with its corresponding number, using low-tack tape and a marker. For a more detailed explanation, see *Basic Techniques*, pages 12–17.

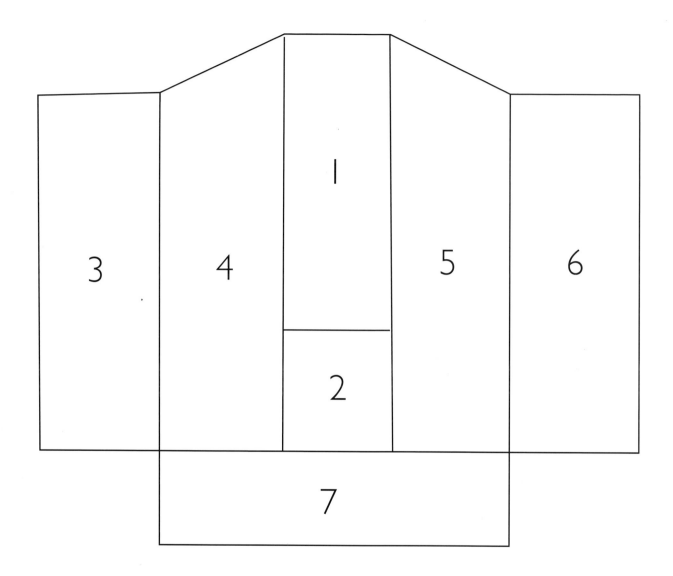

PRAIRIE WINDOW NIGHTLIGHT PATTERN

Copy this pattern at 100% using a photocopier. Make two copies.

Color Key

Use this key to select your glass, or choose your own palette instead. Listed at right are the glass colors used in the project, followed by the corresponding pattern piece numbers.

- *clear beveled: 1*
- *cream opalescent: 2*
- *green opalescent: 4, 5, 7*
- *green hammered: 3, 6*

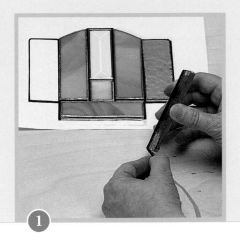

Prepare glass

Cut, grind and label the glass. Wrap each piece of glass with copper foil. Burnish the foil using the side of a pen, pencil or marker.

Tack solder main body and tin wings

Place the pieces on top of the pattern, making sure that the beveled side of the glass faces you. Brush flux onto all copper foil areas. At random points along the seams, tack solder all the pieces of glass together except the two wings. Tin the copper foil surfaces of the two wings.

Solder main body and add decorative soldering

Bead solder the main body together, then tin the perimeter edges. Turn the piece over and solder the reverse side. When finished, return the piece to the front side. Add decorative bead soldering at the top two corners.

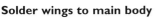

Solder wings to main body

Place the main body, front side up, on a raised wooden block or ceramic tile. Position one wing along the right edge of the main body at a slight downward angle and hold it in place. Apply flux, tack solder the wing to the main body, then secure it by bead soldering along the seam. Turn the piece over and reinforce the seam by soldering it from the reverse side. Secure the left wing using the same process.

Attach plug

With the piece on its back side, align the plug's two brass horizontal tabs with the top seam of the bottom band of glass. Brush the tabs with flux, then secure them to the piece by dropping solder onto the brass and pulling the solder into the existing seam. With a soft, damp cloth, wipe the glass surface clean of any flux.

Midnight Moon
Nightlight

Once you've created one stained glass object, you'll find yourself hooked! If you let the projects on these pages inspire your own original designs, you'll never run out of ideas. Sometimes a single project can generate several wonderful variations. This project, like the one before it, is a nightlight. But as you can tell, the organic feeling of this design, an abstraction of a moon rising over ocean waves, is very different from the rigid geometry of the previous project.

This nightlight fits into any room of the house. The two layers of glass filter and soften the light, allowing the stained glass to cast a quiet glow when the lights go down!

TOOLS AND MATERIALS

- pattern (2 copies)
- wooden work surface
- houschold scissors
- copper foil shears
- glass: yellow muffle, clear ripple, teal streaky, blue streaky (refer to pattern for sizes)
- glass nugget: small light blue cathedral
- spray adhesive
- low-tack or masking tape

- marker
- pistol-grip glass cutter
- grozing pliers
- running pliers
- electric glass grinder
- copper foil, regular and wave
- pen, pencil or marker
- flux brush
- liquid flux

- solder
- soldering iron, with iron station and temperature control
- small wood block or ceramic tile
- nightlight plug (available at stained glass shops)
- soapy water and soft cloth

Preparation

Cut a copy of the pattern apart with household scissors and copper foil shears, spray the glass with adhesive, then affix the individual pattern pieces to the appropriate colored glass. Score the glass along the edges of the adhered paper and break the glass at the score line. Use a glass grinder to smooth out the edges of the glass pieces. Soak the pieces in warm water and remove the paper, then label each piece with its corresponding number, using low-tack tape and a marker. For a more detailed explanation, see *Basic Techniques*, pages 12–17.

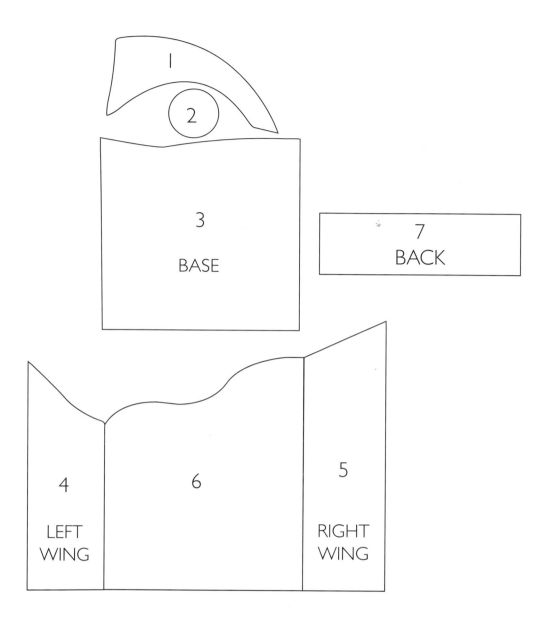

MIDNIGHT MOON PATTERN

Enlarge this pattern by 155% using a photocopier. Make two copies.

Prepare glass

Cut, grind and label the glass. Wrap each piece of glass with copper foil, using the wave foil to wrap all pieces except pieces 1 and 2. Burnish the foil using the side of a pen, pencil or marker.

Apply flux and tin edges

Place the pieces on the work surface, preferably a ceramic tile. With a flux brush, apply flux to all copper foil areas. Tin the copper foil edges of each piece.

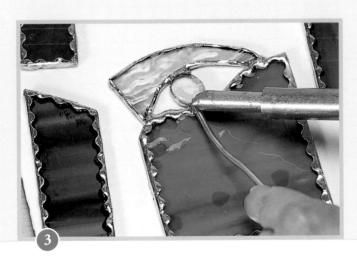

Tack solder base panel

Place pieces 1, 2 and 3 on top of the pattern. Brush flux onto all points of contact between the three pieces, then tack solder them together.

TIP

Droplets or small beads of solder sometimes fall on the stained glass or on your work surface. This solder can be collected and reused. Wait until the solder has cooled, then simply remove the droplets from the surface and put them aside for later use.

Position back piece and align plug

With a soft, damp cloth, wipe the surfaces of the base panel and the back piece. Turn the base panel over and lay the back piece on top of it, about 3/8" (10mm) from the bottom of the base piece, or just enough room for the nightlight plug to be attached. Align the plug's two brass horizontal tabs with the bottom edge of the back piece.

Attach plug

Brush the brass tabs with flux and affix the plug to the back piece by soldering the tabs to the bottom edge. Secure the back piece, with the plug attached, to the base panel by brushing flux along the coinciding edges and soldering.

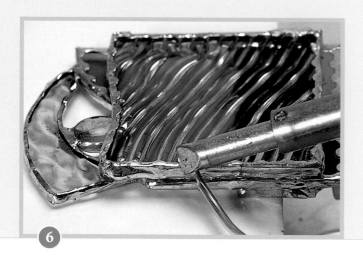

Solder second layer of glass to base panel

Raise the work surface by elevating the ceramic tile a few inches (several centimeters) above the table. Turn the base piece over, allowing the plug to extend off the tile, facing downward. Lay the ripple glass (piece 6) on top of the base panel so that the side edges meet, leaving 3/8" (10mm) of the base showing at the bottom. Brush flux along the coinciding edges and solder to secure the two pieces together.

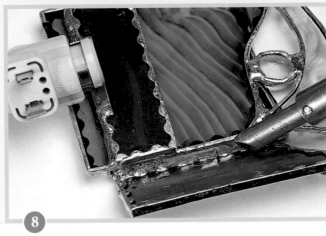

Attach wings

Align the left edge of the base panel with one edge of the ceramic tile. Hold the left wing panel (piece 4) at a 45° angle to the base, pointing downward. Brush flux along the edge where the two pieces meet and tack solder. Secure the right wing panel (piece 5) in the same manner. Bead solder along the edges to secure both wings to the base panel.

Reinforce seams from interior

Turn the piece over so that the wings open toward you. Brush flux along the interior edges where the wings and the base panel meet. Secure the wings from the interior by soldering along the edges. Inspect the piece for any melt-throughs and smooth out any imperfections with the solder and the soldering iron. Use the damp cloth to wipe the glass surface clean of any flux.

TIP

Looking for new and unusual effects with stained glass? You can achieve marvelous results by layering pieces of stained glass on top of one another. This nightlight combines the heavy texture of clear rippled glass with the smooth texture of streaky teal glass. The layers create a filter that diffuses light into a soft, beautiful glow.

Explore the effects of layered color and texture by stacking pieces of glass and holding them up to the light.

Abstract Glass
Landscape

Occasionally you'll come across pieces of glass that have raw, organic edges. In the glass-making process, these irregular ends form as the glass is cooling. While the unrefined appearance may prompt you to discard these pieces, consider their unique qualities before you deem them useless. Sometimes salvaged scrap pieces turn out to be the most valuable!

This project is an example of how random shapes can give rise to an unexpectedly marvelous piece of art. Here, the glass pieces are layered into a dimensional abstract landscape. Instead of hanging this stained glass creation in a window, why not place it on an easel and illuminate it from behind?

TOOLS AND MATERIALS

- pattern (2 copies)
- wooden work surface
- ceramic tile (optional)
- household scissors
- copper foil shears
- glass: cobalt blue opaque, purple streaky, pink streaky, variations of green, scraps of glass with raw edges (refer to pattern for sizes)

- glass nuggets: turquoise, blue or green cathedral (various sizes)
- spray adhesive
- low-tack or masking tape
- marker
- pistol-grip glass cutter
- grozing pliers
- running pliers
- electric glass grinder

- copper foil
- pen, pencil or marker
- flux brush
- liquid flux
- solder
- soldering iron, with iron station and temperature control
- soapy water and soft cloth

Preparation

Cut a copy of the pattern apart with household scissors and copper foil shears, spray the glass with adhesive, then affix the individual pattern pieces to the appropriate colored glass. Score the glass along the edges of the adhered paper and break the glass at the score line. Use a glass grinder to smooth out the edges of the glass pieces. Soak the pieces in warm water and remove the paper, then label each piece with its corresponding number, using low-tack tape and a marker. For a more detailed explanation, see *Basic Techniques*, pages 12–17.

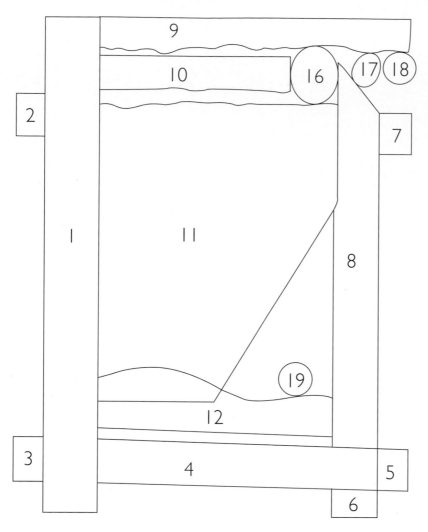

ABSTRACT LANDSCAPE PATTERN

Enlarge this pattern by 180% using a photocopier. Make two copies. Because the raw pieces of glass are irregular, many of the pieces will not match the pattern precisely. As long as all the pieces may be secured together by soldering, absolute precision is not necessary.

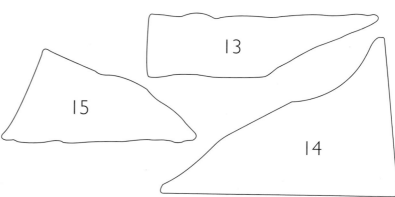

Color Key

Use this key to select your glass, or choose your own palette instead. Listed below are the glass colors used in the project, followed by the corresponding pattern piece numbers.

• *cobalt blue opaque:* 1, 2, 3, 4, 5, 6, 7, 8

• *purple streaky:* 9

• *pink streaky:* 10

• *green variations:* 11, 12, 13, 14, 15

• *turquoise, blue or green nuggets:* 16, 17, 18, 19

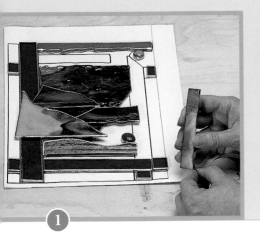

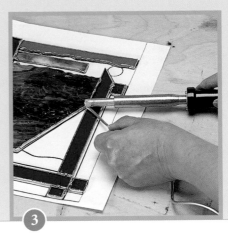

Prepare glass

Cut and grind the glass, leaving raw ends irregular, as desired. Label the glass. Wrap each piece of glass, including the nuggets, with copper foil. Raw ends need not be wrapped. Burnish the copper foil using the side of a pen, pencil or marker. Place the pieces on top of the pattern.

Apply flux and tin edges

Brush flux onto all the copper foil areas. You will have to remove the glass pieces from the pattern to do this since many pieces overlap each other in layers. Tin the copper foil edges on every piece.

Build up layers and secure

Place the bottom layer of glass pieces on top of the pattern. To begin building up the layers, place the large central piece on top of the two vertical side panels. Brush flux onto all areas where the tinned edges meet, then tack solder the pieces in place. Secure pieces to one another by bead soldering along all joints and contact points.

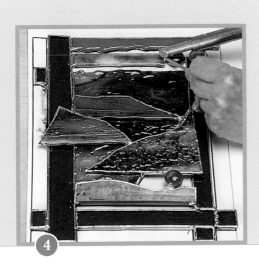

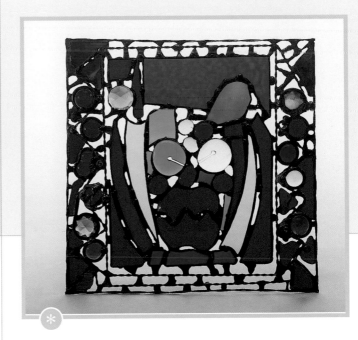

Reinforce and add decorative soldering

Continue to build up layers, always positioning the glass pieces in such a way that they can be secured to other soldered areas in at least two places. Use glass nuggets to bridge any gaps between unsecured areas. Add decorative soldering to provide a finishing touch and to strengthen the seams. Turn the piece over, place supports underneath to keep the surface even, then strengthen the reverse side with additional soldering. Clean with soapy water to remove any flux, then dry with a soft cloth.

ANOTHER IDEA

Compose your own one-of-a-kind masterpiece using scraps, nuggets and small pieces. You may be surprised by the magic that results from a little leftover glass!

Warm
Sunshine Mirror

A sunny stained glass mirror is a welcome addition to any room, lifting the spirits of all who enter. This cheerful sunburst will spread warmth and pizzazz wherever it is displayed. It needs only one thing to make it a complete work of art: the beauty of your own reflection!

The eight holes on the wind chime frame support the beaded wire that meanders around the perimeter, holding the sun rays in place. This ornamental piece is meant to be bright, lighthearted and radiant, so let the spirit of fun guide you!

TOOLS AND MATERIALS

- pattern (multiple copies, as indicated)
- wooden work surface
- household scissors
- glass: yellow–orange–white variation mottled (refer to pattern for sizes)
- spray adhesive
- low-tack or masking tape
- marker
- pistol-grip glass cutter
- grozing pliers
- running pliers

- electric glass grinder
- copper foil
- pen, pencil or marker
- flux brush
- liquid flux
- solder
- soldering iron, with iron station and temperature control
- Kennedy/Kaleidoscope Bead Weaver iron wind chime frame
- 6 lengths of 18-gauge tinned wire, 24" (61cm) each

- 8 lengths of twisted 12-gauge tinned wire, 15" (38cm) each
- wire cutters
- small wood block, approximately 3" x 5" x 1" (8cm x 13cm x 3cm)
- 16–20 decorative glass beads in several shapes and colors, with holes in center
- mirror, cut to fit inside Bead Weaver iron wind chime frame
- clear silicone adhesive sealant, in tube or gun
- soapy water and soft cloth

Preparation

Cut out copies of the pattern pieces with household scissors, spray the glass with adhesive, then affix the pieces to the appropriate colored glass. Score the glass along the edges of the adhered paper and break the glass at the score line. Use a glass grinder to smooth out the edges of the glass pieces. Soak the pieces in warm water and remove the paper, then label each piece with its corresponding number, using low-tack tape and a marker. For a more detailed explanation, see *Basic Techniques*, pages 12–17.

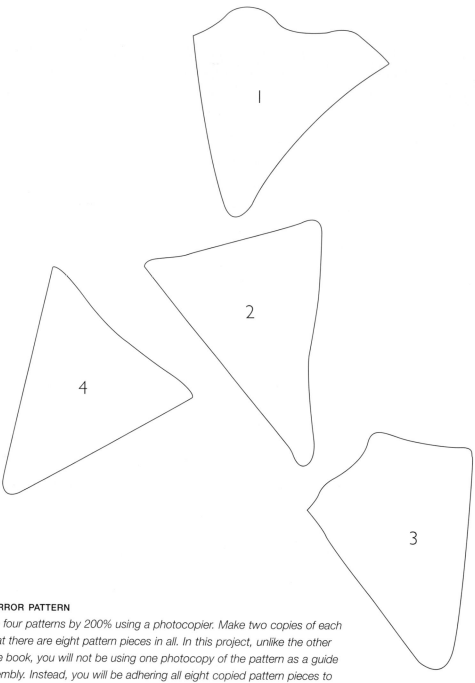

SUNSHINE MIRROR PATTERN

Enlarge these four patterns by 200% using a photocopier. Make two copies of each pattern so that there are eight pattern pieces in all. In this project, unlike the other projects in the book, you will not be using one photocopy of the pattern as a guide for glass assembly. Instead, you will be adhering all eight copied pattern pieces to the glass surface in preparation for scoring and cutting the glass.

Color Key

Use the same glass—yellow–orange–white variation mottled—for all eight pieces.

Prepare glass

Cut, grind and label the glass. Wrap each piece of glass with copper foil. Burnish the copper foil using the side of a pen, pencil or marker.

Apply flux and tin edges

With a flux brush, apply flux to all the copper foil areas. Tin the edges of each piece.

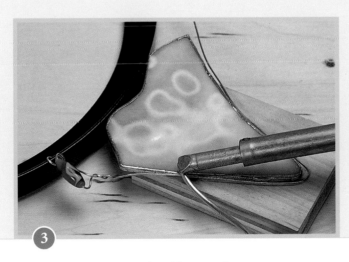

Position sun ray and tack solder to wire

Lay the wind chime flat on the work surface. Run a few inches (several centimeters) of the 24" (61cm) length of 18-gauge tinned wire through one of the small holes on the frame perimeter. Add a glass bead to the wire and secure it by twisting the short end of the wire onto the length. Take glass piece 1 and position it as a sun ray radiating from the perimeter, centering it between the wired frame hole and the next frame hole. Shape the wire to fit along the edge of the glass. Brush flux onto the wire and the tinned edge of the glass. Reduce the heat on the soldering iron to about 80°F (27°C), then tack solder the wire to the piece.

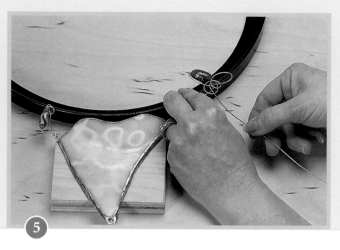

Secure wire to sun ray

Brush more flux onto the tinned edge. With the soldering iron at the same temperature, solder the wire flush to the glass piece, running the soldering iron continuously along the edge of the glass.

Continue pulling wire through perimeter holes

Pull the remaining wire through the next hole, using pliers to pull if necessary, so that the glass piece is taut and not too flimsy. Secure by looping the wire through the hole a few times. Make decorative flourishes by looping and wrapping the wire, adding beads as you go.

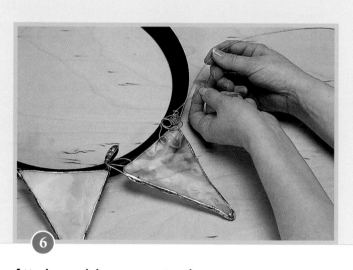

TIP

To keep the wire following closely along the perimeter of the piece, use the head of the pliers to push the wire flush against the edge of the glass.

Attach remaining sun rays to wire

Repeat the process of soldering the sun ray to the wire around the frame, adding the glass pieces in numerical order (1, 2, 3, 4, 1, 2, 3, 4). Be aware of how much wire you have left. Do not finish one piece of wire and begin another on the same piece of glass. If it appears that the remaining length of wire will not extend completely around the sun ray to the next frame hole, secure the wire where it is by looping it through the hole and cutting it, leaving a little extra length with which to make flourishes. Start a new 24" (61 cm) piece of wire, looping it through the same hole a few times and adding a bead. Proceed as before.

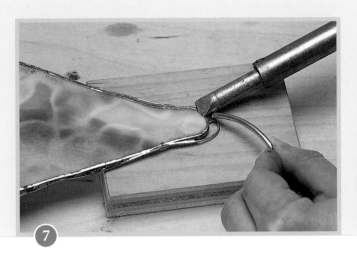 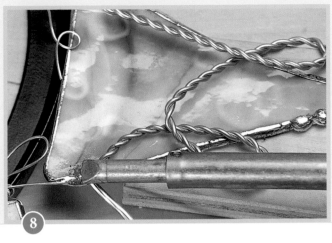

Fill in gaps

After attaching all eight sun rays around the entire perimeter of the frame, tie off the wire at the last hole. Inspect the wire soldered around each piece of glass. If there are any gaps between the wire and the edge of the glass, build up the solder to fill in the gap.

Add decorative wire

Take one 15" (38cm) length of twisted 12-gauge wire (for further instruction on how to twist wire, see *Tip*, page 62). Bend and loop the wire into a decorative shape and lay on top of one of the sun rays. Brush flux onto both ends of the wire, then solder it to the edge of the glass. Secure by soldering at any other points of contact between the wire and the soldered edge. Add decorative bead soldering along the edge of the glass if desired.

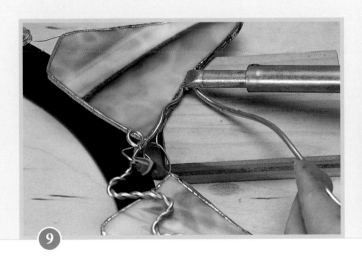 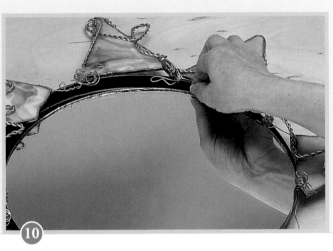

Finish attaching decorative wire

Extend any excess decorative wire to the next sun ray and solder it to the edge. Continue attaching decorative wire to the sun rays until you have worked around the entire perimeter of the frame.

Insert mirror into frame

Apply silicone along the inside lip of the frame. Gently move any beads or wire out of the way, then insert the mirror with its back facing the inner lip. (Alternatively, you can apply silicone along the back perimeter edge of the mirror and then insert the mirror into the frame.) Press down gently to secure, then remove any excess silicone. Let silicone dry. Use a soft, damp cloth to wipe away any flux from the wire and glass surface.

Antique Botanical
Window

Many old stained glass designs offer classic beauty that can be revived in one of your own masterpieces. Next time you are in an environment with stained glass windows, take a moment to study the designs and decide what features are most striking to you. In this botanical panel, basic symmetry creates a quiet, balanced composition that has a timeless quality. Its simplicity makes it a versatile accent to any space.

We took artistic license to slightly alter the color scheme of the original window, which featured a clear background and a green border. This new color scheme is dramatic yet uncomplicated. If you wish, create your own color harmony by selecting three different colors.

TOOLS AND MATERIALS

- pattern (2 copies)
- wooden work surface
- household scissors
- copper foil shears
- glass: cobalt blue cathedral, dark mauve muffle, green streaky (refer to pattern for sizes)
- spray adhesive
- low-tack or masking tape

- marker
- pistol-grip glass cutter
- grozing pliers
- running pliers
- electric glass grinder
- copper foil
- pen, pencil or marker
- T-square
- flux brush

- liquid flux
- solder
- soldering iron, with iron station and temperature control
- 5' (1.5m) zinc U-channel, 3/8" (10mm) width
- 2 brass hangers
- patina
- soapy water and soft cloth

Preparation

Cut a copy of the pattern apart with household scissors and copper foil shears, spray the glass with adhesive, then affix the individual pattern pieces to the appropriate colored glass. Score the glass along the edges of the adhered paper and break the glass at the score line. Use a glass grinder to smooth out the edges of the glass pieces. Soak the pieces in warm water and remove the paper, then label each piece with its corresponding number, using low-tack tape and a marker. For a more detailed explanation, see *Basic Techniques*, pages 12–17.

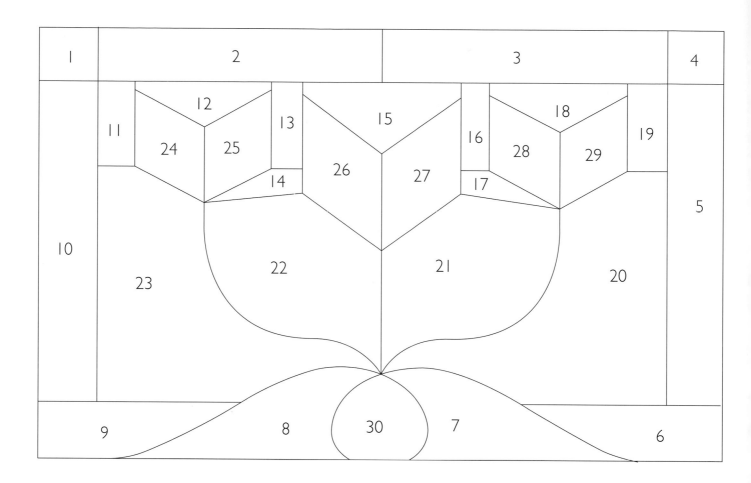

ANTIQUE BOTANICAL PATTERN

Enlarge this pattern by 222% using a photocopier. Make two copies. (Some photocopiers only enlarge up to 200%. If this is the case, make a copy of the pattern at 200%, then photocopy that copy at 111%.)

Color Key

Use this key to select your glass, or choose your own palette instead. Listed at right are the glass colors used in the project, followed by the corresponding pattern piece numbers.

- **cobalt blue cathedral:** 1, 2, 3, 4, 5, 6, 7, 8, 9, 10
- **dark mauve muffle:** 11, 12, 13, 14, 15, 16, 17, 18, 19, 20, 21, 22, 23
- **green streaky:** 24, 25, 26, 27, 28, 29, 30

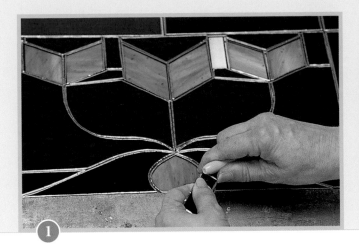

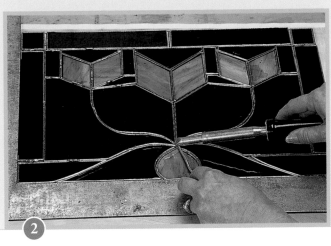

Prepare glass

Cut, grind and label the glass. Wrap each piece of glass with copper foil. Burnish the foil using the side of a pen, pencil or marker. Position the glass pieces on top of the pattern.

Apply flux and tack solder

Use a T-square to line up the outside edges at right angles. With a flux brush, apply flux to all copper foil areas except the perimeter edge. Tack solder at random points along the copper foil seams until all the pieces are joined together.

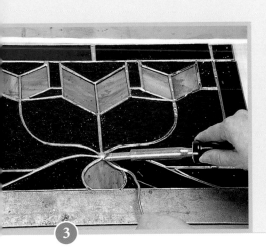

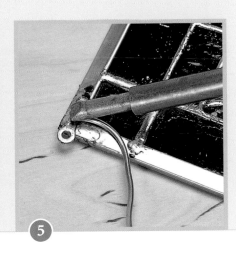

Solder

Secure the pieces together by bead soldering along all the seams. Stop soldering ¼" (6mm) from the outside edge to allow space for the frame. Turn the piece over. Flat solder the reverse side, again leaving ¼" (6mm) around the edge to accommodate the frame.

Secure piece in frame

Cut four lengths of zinc U-channel to fit around the perimeter. Fit each side of the glass into the channel. Brush flux onto the corners of the frame and on all points where the soldered seams meet the zinc frame. Solder the corners together, then solder all points of contact between the seams and the frame. Turn the piece over and repeat the process on the reverse side.

Attach hangers

Apply flux and tin the hangers. Lay the hangers along the frame at the top back corners so that the hooks extend just beyond the top edge. Brush flux onto the hangers and the corners, then solder a hanger to each corner. Clean the piece with soapy water to remove any flux and dry with a soft cloth. If desired, apply patina to soldered areas, following the instructions on the package. Clean again with warm, soapy water, then dry.

Coiled Candleholder

Debra Neace designed this fabulous contemporary candleholder, which gives stained glass an unexpected twist by incorporating beads, coiled wire and open-sided walls. Candlelight will look beautiful sparkling through the opalescent glass, creating a romantic atmosphere with a soft ambient glow.

As you become more comfortable with the stained glass process, feel free to experiment with the different tools and materials that are currently available. In this project, we have suggested trying silvered foil instead of copper foil. Silvered foil has a silver coating, which resembles the finish of solder. Otherwise, the two kinds of adhesive tape are identical. Sometimes it is fun to just try something new!

TOOLS AND MATERIALS

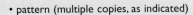

- pattern (multiple copies, as indicated)
- wooden work surface
- household scissors
- copper foil shears
- glass: white iridized opalescent (refer to pattern for sizes)
- spray adhesive
- low-tack or masking tape
- marker
- pistol-grip glass cutter

- grozing pliers
- running pliers
- electric glass grinder
- silvered foil (or copper foil)
- pen, pencil or marker
- flux brush
- liquid flux
- solder
- soldering iron, with iron station and temperature control

- 4 lengths of 12- to 14-gauge tinned wire, 30" (76cm) each
- wire cutters
- 20 decorative glass beads in several shapes and colors, with holes in center
- small wood block
- soapy water and soft cloth
- pillar candle, 4" (10cm) tall

Preparation

Cut a copy of the pattern apart with household scissors and copper foil shears, spray the glass with adhesive, then affix the individual pattern pieces to the appropriate colored glass. Score the glass along the edges of the adhered paper and break the glass at the score line. Use a glass grinder to smooth out the edges of the glass pieces. Soak the pieces in warm water and remove the paper, then label each piece with its corresponding number, using low-tack tape and a marker. For a more detailed explanation, see *Basic Techniques*, pages 12–17.

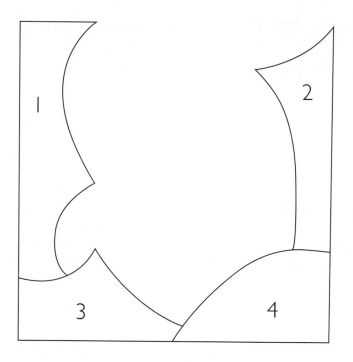

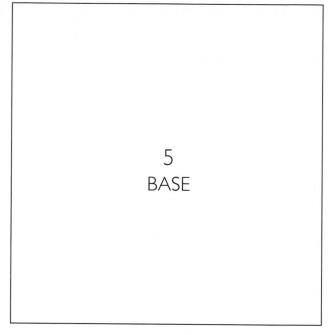

CANDLEHOLDER SIDE PATTERN

Enlarge this pattern by 155% using a photocopier. Make eight copies, then label two sets as A, two sets as B, two sets as C and two sets as D.

CANDLEHOLDER BASE PATTERN

Enlarge this pattern by 155% using a photocopier. Make one copy, then label as Base.

❋

Color Key
All of the glass pieces in this project are white iridized opalescent.

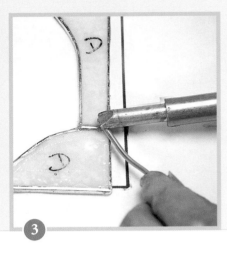

Prepare glass

Cut and grind the glass. Divide the glass into four sets, labeled A, B, C and D. Each set represents one side of the cube. Wrap each piece of glass, including the base piece, with silvered foil. Burnish the foil using the side of a pen, pencil or marker.

Apply flux and tack solder

With a flux brush, apply flux to all foil areas on the base piece, then tin the edges. Brush flux onto the foil areas of all four pieces in one set, then tin those edges. Place the four pieces on top of the side pattern. Tack solder each seam together to keep the pieces in place.

Solder

Turn the soldering heat down to 80°F. (27°C). Secure the pieces by soldering all the foil seams together. Turn the piece over and solder the reverse side. Repeat this process for the three other sets of pieces until you have four complete sides.

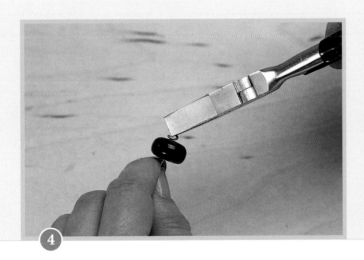

String bead

String a decorative bead on the end of a 30" (76cm) length of wire. Twist the end of the wire a few times into a hook to keep the bead from falling off.

Create coils

Twist the wire around a marker to create a corkscrew effect. Stop coiling periodically and add another bead. Continue until you have added four or five beads and your wire is completely coiled.

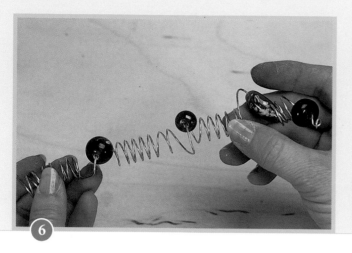

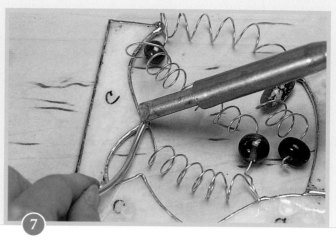

Stretch wire

Gently pull the coil apart so that it stretches out a bit.

Attach coiled wire to one side

Lay one side flat on the work surface. Position the coil within the interior opening of the piece so that it runs from one interior point to another. Brush flux onto the points. Solder one end of the wire to one of the upper corners, then move down, continuing to solder the wire at different contact points until it is secured to the glass.

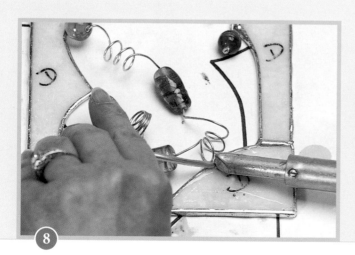

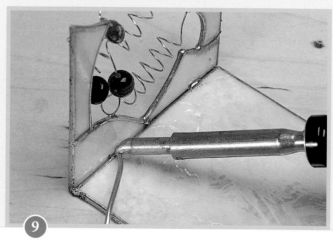

Attach coiled wire to remaining sides

Repeat the process with the other three sides, making sure that the coiled wire is secured to each piece of glass.

Attach one side piece to base piece

Lay the base piece flat on the work surface. Hold one of the side pieces at a 90° angle to the base piece. Brush flux along the coinciding interior edge where the two pieces meet. Tack solder the inside seam to join the two pieces, then secure by bead soldering them together along the seam.

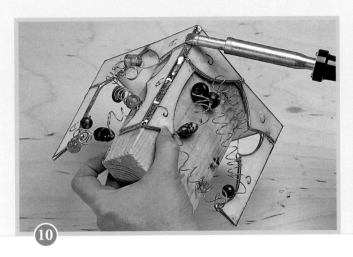

Attach remaining side panels

Hold a second side piece in place at a 90° angle to the two attached pieces. Brush flux along the exterior seams. Tack solder the seams, then secure the pieces together by bead soldering.

Solder interior seams

Brush flux on the interior seam, then reinforce it by soldering. Repeat the process with the remaining side panels until all four sides are secure. When you get to the final side, access the interior base seam by laying the cube on its side, gently propped up. Extend the soldering iron inside and solder along the seam.

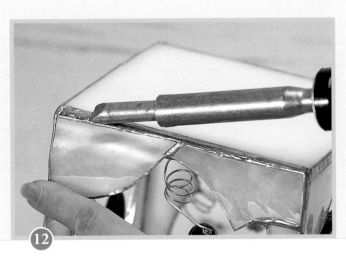

TIP

Hold a small wood block inside the corner joint as you solder the exterior seams. This will act as a support while you work and it will also prevent hot solder from slipping through the seams.

Reinforce base seams

Turn the cube over and reinforce the base by soldering along the exterior seams. Wash the glass with a soft, damp cloth to remove any flux. When the piece is complete, place a pillar candle inside.

Resources

✱ Supplies

Tools and materials for stained glass projects are available at many craft and hobby stores and almost all stained glass shops. Check your local yellow pages for shops near you.

Kaleidoscope Stained Glass
704 Main Street
Covington, KY 41011
Phone: (859) 491-2222
www.stainedglass4you.com
Glass, supplies, books, patterns, Kennedy/Kaleidoscope wind chime frames and garden stake frames

✱ Organizations

Art Glass Association
P. O. Box 2537
Zanesville, OH 43702-2537
Phone: (740) 454-1194
Toll Free: (866) 301-2421
Fax: (740) 454-1194
www.artglassassociation.com
Association of glass artists, retailers, studios, suppliers and hobbyists, to promote awareness, knowledge and involvement for the growth of the art glass industry

International Guild of Glass Artists, Inc.
www.igga.org
International nonprofit association of glass artists, artisans and craftspeople with the mission to facilitate communication among glass artists, to encourage education and promote excellence in the glass arts

Stained Glass Association of America
10009 East 62nd Street
Raytown, MO 64133
Phone: (800) 438-7422
www.stainedglass.org
sgaa@stainedglass.org
Nonprofit association to promote the development and advancement of the stained and decorative art glass craft

Index

The Best in
Creative Crafting

is from North Light Books!

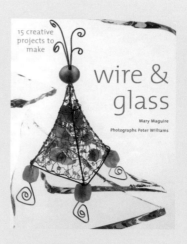

Discover the creative potential of wire and glass! The array of unique projects found inside, from mirror frames to fire screens, are inexpensive to create with no special skills or elaborate tools required.

Detailed directions and full-color photos guide you every step of the way from concept to completion for beautiful home décor items.

ISBN 1-58180-199-8, paperback, 112 pages, #31976-K

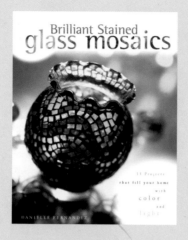

Combine two popular crafts into one exciting art form! Inside this book you'll discover simple mosaic techniques that can be used to create stunning, sophisticated designs for both home and garden décor. From windows and vases to picture frames and light fixtures, you'll find step-by-step instructions for gorgeous projects that come to life when illuminated by candlelight, incandescent or natural light.

ISBN 1-58180-185-8, paperback, 128 pages, #31955-K

You can create gorgeous home decor and garden art using today's new, craft-friendly metals, meshes and wire. You'll find 15 projects, ranging from lamps to picture frames. Most can be completed in an afternoon!

ISBN 1-58180-330-3, paperback, 96 pages, #32296-K

Bring a dash of color to windows, doors and household glassware with this comprehensive and enjoyable guide. 20 step-by-step projects and 100 trace-off patterns allow you to employ a variety of glass painting techniques for beautiful results every time.

ISBN 0-7153-1611-7, paperback, 128 pages, #41531-K

These and other fine North Light titles are available from your local art & craft retailer, bookstore, online supplier or by calling 1-800-448-0915.